T0358330

Cambridge Elements ☰

Elements in Musical Theatre
edited by
William A. Everett
University of Missouri-Kansas City

SINGING *ZARZUELA*, 1896–1958

Approaching Portamento and Musical Expression through Historical Recordings

Eva Moreda Rodríguez
University of Glasgow

CAMBRIDGE
UNIVERSITY PRESS

Shaftesbury Road, Cambridge CB2 8EA, United Kingdom

One Liberty Plaza, 20th Floor, New York, NY 10006, USA

477 Williamstown Road, Port Melbourne, VIC 3207, Australia

314–321, 3rd Floor, Plot 3, Splendor Forum, Jasola District Centre,
New Delhi – 110025, India

103 Penang Road, #05–06/07, Visioncrest Commercial, Singapore 238467

Cambridge University Press is part of Cambridge University Press & Assessment,
a department of the University of Cambridge.

We share the University's mission to contribute to society through the pursuit of
education, learning and research at the highest international levels of excellence.

www.cambridge.org
Information on this title: www.cambridge.org/9781009475747

DOI: 10.1017/9781009419239

First published 2024

A catalogue record for this publication is available from the British Library

ISBN 978-1-009-47574-7 Hardback
ISBN 978-1-009-41924-6 Paperback
ISSN 2631-6528 (online)
ISSN 2631-651X (print)

Singing *Zarzuela*, 1896–1958

Approaching Portamento and Musical Expression through Historical Recordings

Elements in Musical Theatre

DOI: 10.1017/9781009419239
First published online: December 2024

Eva Moreda Rodríguez
University of Glasgow

Author for correspondence: Eva Moreda Rodríguez,
Eva.MoredaRodriguez@glasgow.ac.uk

Abstract: In the last few years, digitizations and reissues of historical recordings of Spanish *zarzuela* – from wax cylinders in the 1890s to long-play records in the 1950s – have revealed a range of contrasting vocal performance styles. By focusing on portamento, this Element sets the foundations for a contextually sensitive history of vocal performance practices in *zarzuela*. It takes stock of technological changes and shifts in commercial strategies and listening habits to reveal what the recorded evidence tells us about the historical development of portamento practices and considers how these findings can allow us to reconstruct the expressive code of *zarzuela* as it was performed in the late nineteenth century and how it transformed itself throughout the next half century. These transformations are contextualized alongside other changes, including the make-up of audiences, the discourses about the genre's connection to national identity and the influence of other musical-theatrical genres and languages.

Keywords: *Zarzuela*, 19th-century singing performance practice, Portamento, Historical recordings

ISBNs: 9781009475747 (HB), 9781009419246 (PB), 9781009419239 (OC)
ISSNs: 2631-6528 (online), 2631-651X (print)

Contents

Introduction

When listening to recordings of vocal and instrumental works made around 1900, our attention is likely to be drawn, for better or worse, to portamento. Instances of portamento in these recordings are indeed considerably greater than we would hear in present-day performances of the same works. From our modern perspective, we may regard these earlier interpretations as being overly sentimental or kitsch. *Zarzuela*, the Spanish-language musical theatre genre that flourished between 1850 and 1950, was no exception.[1] This becomes obvious from even cursory listening to the increasing number of historical recordings that have become widely available in recent years, both through digitization projects led by research libraries[2] and through commercial CD releases.[3]

The appearance of this wealth of material has the potential to transform the ways in which we study and understand *zarzuela*, including how it was interwoven into its cultural and social contexts and assessing its place within broader styles of singing and their developments between the late nineteenth and mid twentieth centuries. Scholarship on *zarzuela* has grown significantly since the 1980s, after musicology established itself as a discipline in its own right within Spanish academia and *zarzuela* became one of its pre-eminent objects of study. Out of necessity, much of the work conducted in the initial decades was foundational and was led to a great extent by the Instituto Complutense de Ciencias Musicales (Complutense Institute of Musical Sciences) at the Universidad Complutense de Madrid. Staff at the Instituto compiled an ambitious dictionary (*Diccionario de la zarzuela en España e Hispanoamérica*) that included entries on composers, works and singers,[4] published biographies of the

---

[1] Baroque *zarzuela* developed between the 1630s and 1750s as a Spanish-language musical theatre genre. The revival of *zarzuela* in the mid nineteenth century in the hands of Francisco Asenjo Barbieri and others was conceptually rooted in these earlier *zarzuelas* in an attempt to build a Spanish-language theatrical genre. Musically, however, they did not look back to the Spanish Baroque but rather to contemporary Italian opera and French *opéra comique* and *opérette*.

[2] The most significant digital collections are those of the Biblioteca Nacional de España (available through the Biblioteca Digital Hispánica, www.bne.es/es/Catalogos/BibliotecaDigitalHispanica/Inicio/index.html), which has digitized 20,000 historical recordings (including wax cylinders, shellac discs and piano rolls), and the Biblioteca de Catalunya (available at Memòria Digital de Catalunya, https://mdc1.csuc.cat), which has digitized more than 300 cylinders (including about 50 of *zarzuela*) made by the Barcelona industrialist Ruperto Regordosa in his own home in the early twentieth century. Eresbil – Archivo de la Música Vasca is home to about 500 cylinders, most of which have been digitized, but as of February 2024 these can only be listened to on-site, though a small number are available online (www.eresbil.eus/web/ybarra/presentacion.aspx). A small number of *zarzuela* recordings are also available at digitized collections outside Spain (e.g., the Irvin S. Gilmore Library at Yale University).

[3] These include those available on Blue Moon Serie Lírica and Naxos Classical Archives.

[4] Emilio Casares Rodicio, ed., *Diccionario de la zarzuela en España e Hispanoamérica* (Madrid: Instituto Complutense de Ciencias Musicales, 2006), 2 vols.

main composers of the genre[5] and launched a series of editions that included some of the best-known repertoire works (*Colección Música Hispánica – Música lírica*). At a later stage – and more within the field of Spanish cultural studies rather than musicology – new research directions pushed the study of the genre beyond the 'composers-and-work' paradigm and focused on its cultural, social, political and ideological dimensions, such as the place of *zarzuela* within discourses of national identity and studies on venues and audiences.[6]

The realm of *zarzuela* performance, however, has remained surprisingly unexplored. Studies of the social and cultural history of performers[7] and particularly of performance practice remain limited.[8] This is somewhat para-doxical. Presumably, a main reason why audiences kept filling *zarzuela* theatres was because of the fascination that the music, as conveyed in the act of performance, exerted on them. Yet we know little about the sonic means through which audiences perceived *zarzuelas* and their associated discourses and connotations.

Against this backdrop, this Element intends to set the foundations for a contextually sensitive history of vocal performance practices in recorded *zarzuela* by tracing the story, from the late nineteenth to the mid-twentieth centuries, of one of the most conspicuous features heard in these early

---

[5] Luis G. Iberni, ed., *Ruperto Chapí: Memorias y escritos* (Madrid: Instituto Complutense de Ciencias Musicales, 1995); Víctor Sánchez, *Tomás Bretón: Un músico de la Restauración* (Madrid: Instituto Complutense de Ciencias Musicales, 2002); María Encina Cortizo, *Emilio Arrieta: De la ópera a la zarzuela* (Madrid: Instituto Complutense de Ciencias Musicales, 1998); Emilio Casares Rodicio, *Francisco Asenjo Barbieri: el hombre y el creador* (Madrid: Editorial Complutense, 1994).

[6] Lucy Harney, 'Controlling Resistance, Resisting Control: The *género chico* and the Dynamics of Mass Entertainment in Late Nineteenth-Century Spain', *Arizona Journal of Hispanic Cultural Studies* 10 (2006): 151–167; Enrique Encabo, *Música y nacionalismos en España* (Barcelona: Erasmus, 2006); Lucy D. Harney, '*Zarzuela* and the Pastoral', *Hispanic Issue* 12, no. 8 (2008): 252–273; Tobias Brandenberger and Antje Dreyer, eds., *La zarzuela y sus caminos: Del siglo XVII a la actualidad* (Berlin: Lit, 2016); Andrea García Torres, 'El teatro lírico como género difusor de las ideologías dominantes en torno a la Guerra de África (1859–1860)', *Anuario Musical* 72 (2017): 191–208.

[7] While a significant number of performers' biographies exist that provide very valuable informa-tion, most if not all are more journalistic or reminiscent than scholarly in nature. See, for example, Olimpio Arca Caldas, *Unha voz … Mary Isaura* (A Estrada: Asociación Fillos e Amigos da Estrada, 2001); Pedro Gómez Manzanares, *Felisa Herrero: Musa de la zarzuela* (Madrid: Cultiva Libros, 2011); María Luz González Peña, Javier Suárez-Pajares and Julio Arce Bueno, *Mujeres de la escena 1900–1940* (Madrid: SGAE, 1996); José Manuel Rodríguez Arnáez, *Lucrecia Arana: Jarrera castiza – La reina de las tiples del género chico* (Haro: Asociación Cultural Manuel Bartolomé Cossío, 1992).

[8] The only works that specifically address singing practices are Ramón Regidor Arribas, *La voz en la zarzuela* (Madrid: Real Musical, 1991) and the dictionary entry 'Voz', in Emilio Casares Rodicio, ed., *Diccionario de la zarzuela en España e Hispanoamérica* (Madrid: Instituto Complutense de Ciencias Musicales, 2006), vol. 2, 941–944. Both focus mostly on voice types and sub-types and matters of range and tessitura and take a prescriptive rather than descriptive approach. The use of historical primary sources other than the scores themselves is limited.

recordings: portamento. The start and finish dates frame a cohesive unit within the history of recorded music in Spain. In 1896, the first commercial recordings of *zarzuela* in Spain are likely to have been made and in 1958, Ataúlfo Argenta, a prolific conductor who pioneered the recording of complete *zarzuelas* on LPs (long-playing 33 rpm records), passed away. While *zarzuelas* certainly continued to be recorded after 1958, Argenta's death marked, in a way, the end of an era. The 1950s also brought fundamental changes to the genre's popularity on stage. Once a thriving art form filled with premieres of new works, by the end of the decade *zarzuela* had become increasingly fossilized into a set repertoire of canonic works, a process to which Argenta's extensive catalogue contributed considerably.

Portamento is certainly not the only aspect of performance in earlier *zarzuela* that merits attention, but it is particularly important because it offers a compelling way to hear the interweaving of performance style with the genre's social and cultural contexts. This can allow us to explore how and why styles can change according to social and cultural shifts without resorting to simplistic cause-effect explanations. One particular aspect of portamento that allows us to combine performance practice with contextual study in this way is that it was an aspect of performance that *zarzuela* shared with contemporaneous recorded genres, including opera, art song, various vernacular vocal styles and a wealth of instrumental music. This necessitates that we engage with questions such as how *zarzuela* interfaced and interacted with these other genres, both in Spain and internationally, how these interactions were regarded by composers, musicians, critics and audiences at different points in time and, ultimately, how the genre was perceived to represent national identity in a distinctive way. These are indeed key questions in *zarzuela* scholarship that go beyond performance. While the genre was universally recognized as a distinctively Spanish art form, a range of controversies and debates emerged throughout the decades on the extent to which foreign influences were to be either celebrated or decried.[9]

While some of these controversies and debates will be spelled out in more detail throughout this Element, there are two general themes in the reception of *zarzuela* in Spain that I wish to call attention to at this point, for they provide a foundation for understanding much of the history of the genre, particularly to newcomers. First, the discourses of Spanish identity upon which *zarzuela* was built and which it disseminated to its audiences were not monolithic. Different notions of Spanishness coexist in *zarzuela* and perceptions and debates concerning Spanish national identity changed throughout the period under study. Second, controversies abound surrounding the relationship between *zarzuela*

---

[9] Sánchez, *Tomás Bretón*, 243.

and opera. While the two genres obviously share a great deal in terms of compositional techniques and singing styles, some in the Spanish music scene at different points in time have regarded *zarzuela* as inimical to opera, arguing that Spanish composers had been drawn to *zarzuela* because it was popular and profitable. By writing *zarzuela*, it was thought that they were neglecting to build a tradition of Spanish opera, one that would allegedly have given Spanish music a more universal appeal.[10]

Apart from disentangling the complex threads of Spanish national identity, *zarzuela* and opera, focusing on the study of recorded portamento also allows us to examine how performance practice was interwoven into the history of recording technologies and indeed into the recording industry itself. In order to explore the interface between individual performance practices and the relevant technological conditions, this Element, rather than focusing on a small number of well-known performers (as has often been the case with earlier studies of performance practice as reflected in early recordings), engages with an ample number of singers from various backgrounds. These recordings often reflect what a majority of contemporary *zarzuela* critics, audience members and singers may have considered less-than-optimal performance decisions. Such choices, as we will see, can often be chalked down to a lack of experience or expertise on the part of the recordist or of the singer, particularly in the latter's dealings with technology.[11] Rather than simply dismissing these moments as unrepresentative, this Element regards them as opportunities to consider how Spanish recordists and singers interacted and experimented with the parade of successive new technologies arriving in the country. These interfaces and experiments sometimes influenced performance practices on stage in what Mark Katz has termed the 'phonograph effect'. In such instances, recording technologies do not simply document stage performance practices but rather reflect changes in performing styles that happened in the recording studio and subsequently became commonplace in live performance.[12]

---

[10] On the issue of *zarzuela* versus Spanish opera, see Clinton D. Young, 'Why Did Spain Fail to Develop Nationalist Opera?', *Bulletin for Spanish and Portuguese Historical Studies* 38, no. 1 (2013): 117–137, especially 117–118 and 137; Elena Torres, 'Zarzuela y musicología: historia de un debate en permanente revisión', in Alberto González Lapuente and Alberto Honrado Pinilla, eds., *Horizontes de la zarzuela* (Madrid: Fundación Jacinto e Inocencio Guerrero, 2014), 45–59, especially 46–47.

[11] Summaries of a range of technical issues of this nature can be found in Daniel Leech-Wilkinson, 'Understanding the Sources: Performances and Recordings', in *The Changing Sound of Music* (London: CHARM, 2009), www.charm.rhul.ac.uk/studies/chapters/chap3.html and Neal Peres da Costa, *Off the Record: Performing Practices in Romantic Piano Playing* (New York: Oxford University Press, 2012), 4–41.

[12] Mark Katz, *Capturing Sound: How Technology Has Changed Music* (Berkeley, CA: University of California Press, 2010), 102.

Beyond looking at the impact of recording technologies on performance practice, focusing on the early recording industry also allows the exploration of related topics that go beyond the merely technological, including, for example, the impact of recording technologies on the music profession as well as on listening and consumption practices.[13] The formats and conventions we hear in early recordings – particularly those that might seem more alien to us – also allow us to consider broader questions pertaining to ontologies of recorded music vis-à-vis live performance, listening practices and the circulation of recorded music. In turn, we can analyse how these dimensions may have panned out in distinct ways within the context of Spain and *zarzuela*, thus contributing to the shaping of discourses surrounding national identity. However, while *zarzuela* enjoyed a significant degree of circulation in the Americas (in both live and recorded formats), recordings were primarily made in Spain. (Exceptions will be noted and discussed in due course.) Focusing on Spanish-made *zarzuela* recordings facilitates the comparison between recordings that essentially came from the same milieu and which were closely connected to the genre's vibrant live culture, at least until its decline in popularity.

Interpreting Portamento through *Zarzuela* Recordings

This Element takes as its starting point the fact that portamento in *zarzuela* did not develop in isolation from other vocal genres. Of these, opera and art song are the only ones that have thus far received sustained scholarly attention and this scholarship informs the present enquiry. The connection between *zarzuela* and other sung genres is confirmed by historical evidence; indeed, the origins of modern *zarzuela* in the mid nineteenth century were decisively influenced by Italian *bel canto* and French *opéra comique* and *opérette*, not just in terms of compositional language but also performance practice. *Zarzuela* singers at that time trained either at the Real Conservatorio de Madrid or privately with opera-focused singing teachers, many of whom were Italian.[14] Throughout the history

---

[13] See also works coming from cultural studies and the sociology of music such as Stefan Gauß, 'Listening to the Horn: On the Cultural History of the Phonograph and the Gramophone', in Daniel Morat, ed., *Sounds of Modern History: Auditory Cultures in 19th- and 20th-Century Europe* (Oxford: Berghahn, 2014), 71–100, especially 81; Arved Ashby, *Absolute Music, Mechanical Reproduction* (Oakland, CA: University of California Press, 2010), 30; and Patrick Feaster, '"Rise and Obey the Command": Performative Fidelity and the Exercise of Phonographic Power', *Journal of Popular Music Studies* 24, no. 3 (2012): 357–395, especially 358–359.

[14] Emilio Cotarelo y Mori, *Historia de la zarzuela* (Madrid: Instituto Complutense de Ciencias Musicales, 2001), 165–72; María del Coral Morales Villar, 'Los tratados de canto en España durante el siglo XIX: Técnica vocal e interpretación de la música lírica' (PhD thesis, University of Granada, 2008), 256–264.

of the genre, it was not unheard of for singers to move back and forth between *zarzuela* and opera, which suggests that singing practices were thought to be transferable, at least to an extent, between the genres.

Evidence suggests, however, that performance practices, though transferable, might not have been thought to be exactly equivalent, for *zarzuela* could also accommodate numbers with more traditional or popular streaks. These songs presumably called for performing styles more akin to those heard in music hall, cabaret and similar urban genres that were being recorded elsewhere at the turn of the century. Such vocal deliveries were characterized by a low soft palate that resulted in a nasal tone and intelligible diction, both of which were key to making humorous texts intelligible.

Similarly, when leading opera singers ventured into *zarzuela*, their approaches to singing could sometimes raise eyebrows. The Teatro Real in Madrid, although specializing in opera, occasionally hosted one-off perform-ances of successful *zarzuelas* outside the main season. Some roles went to well-known *zarzuela* performers and others to operatic celebrities. In 1904, Ruperto Chapí's *La revoltosa* was staged with opera stars Matilde Lerma, Andrés Perelló de Segurola, Luisa García Rubio and Emilio Cabello in the main roles. Only one *zarzuela* performer appeared with them, the baritone Emilio Mesejo, who at the time was immensely popular. Reviews of these performances at the Real document certain performance practices that we do not normally hear in recordings or find in other reviews. Lerma allegedly interpolated a high C in a duet that was said to 'leave her partner, Mesejo, speechless and shocked'.[15] *Zarzuela* was seen as being able to integrate such hybrid elements into itself, unlike opera.

The definition of portamento employed in this Element is deliberately a simple one: following Ellen T. Harris in *The Grove Dictionary of Music and Musicians*, it can be thought of as 'the connection of two notes passing audibly through the intervening pitches'.[16] This definition is well suited to the period under study and aptly describes what we hear in *zarzuela* recordings. While in the eighteenth century and earlier the notion of *portamento di voce* was broad and vague, by the early nineteenth century its meaning had been restricted to the expressive sliding which is familiar to us today.[17] Within *zarzuela* recordings – as well as in contemporary examples from other genres – portamento reflects some variability, for example, in terms of speed or the size

---

[15] 'Teatro Real', *El Heraldo de Madrid*, 25 January 1904. All translations are mine.

[16] Ellen T. Harris, 'Portamento (i)'. Grove Music Online, www.oxfordmusiconline.com/grovemusic/view/10.1093/gmo/9781561592630.001.0001/omo-9781561592630-e-0000040990, accessed 14 July 2023.

[17] Potter, 'The Rise and Fall of Portamento', 524–526.

of the intervals to which it was applied. This Element will examine how this variability maps out over time and what factors might have shaped its different directions.

Several conclusions drawn from existing scholarship on portamento inform my approach to *zarzuela* recordings. First, a key preoccupation in many studies has been to deduce from existing recordings the rules that might have determined when and how portamento should have or could have been applied.[18] Written sources, such as treatises and reviews, do not always help in this regard. Sometimes they may warn against performing portamento in ways that go against good taste, but rarely do they define what is meant by good taste. This is seen in Spanish sources from the period at hand[19] as well as in others from throughout Europe.[20] Our modern ears, unaccustomed as they typically are to portamento, might be unreliable in determining what constituted good taste at the time and what did not. On the basis of recordings, a range of literature has convincingly mapped out portamento conventions, for example, within the boundaries of a composer's output,[21] a single song[22] or a particular country.[23] My approach here follows a similar logic: given that portamento conventions were not spelled out – at least in writing – our best means to understand how they worked is to compare a manageable body of recordings that share a common notion of style. While outliers and unorthodox practices certainly made their way into recordings, such comparisons can help us identify norms and exceptions and detailed examinations of the historical contexts can assist in understanding how these practices came about and what they reveal about the relationships of singers, listeners and recordists to technology.

Another result of earlier studies relevant to the present one concerns the relationship between portamento and legato. Scholars have repeatedly pointed out that portamento is not only a deliberate expressive choice in musically or dramatically important moments but also can operate as a technical aid to facilitate legato (smooth) motion on difficult or large intervals.[24] Spanish primary sources explicitly recognize that portamento had this dual nature.

---

[18] Deborah Kauffman, 'Portamento in Romantic Opera', *Performance Practice Review* 5, no. 2 (1992): 139–158; John Potter, 'Beggar at the Door: The Rise and Fall of Portamento in Singing', *Music and Letters* 87, no. 4 (2006): 523–550.

[19] Morales Villar, *Los tratados de canto en España*, 373 and 454.

[20] Potter, 'Beggar at the Door', 523.

[21] Roger Freitas, 'Towards a Verdian Ideal of Singing: Emancipation from Modern Orthodoxy', *Journal of the Royal Musical Association* 127, no. 2 (2002): 226–257, especially 244.

[22] Potter, 'Beggar at the Door', 525–532.

[23] Sarah Potter, 'Changing Vocal Style and Technique in Britain during the Long Nineteenth Century' (PhD thesis, University of Leeds, 2014), 109–113.

[24] Kauffman, 'Portamento in Romantic Opera', 153.

José Aranguren's *Prontuario del cantante e instrumentista* (1860) states that portamento could be used merely as an aide to achieve legato between syllables, though it could be exaggerated and thus become an intentional expressive device.[25] The legato function of portamento can be regarded as part of what Roberta Plack has labelled 'vocal habits', that is, the default way in which a singer approaches her instrument before adding any intentional expressive affects.[26] A singer's vocal habits, or defaults, are determined by technical and physiological factors (e.g., a singer's age and her ability to move from one pitch to another with or without having to resort to audible portamento) as well as conventions of technique and style in fashion at any given time.[27] Again, comparisons between recordings and examinations of portamento within the context of other aspects of vocal performance are useful in clarifying where the boundary might lie between vocal habit and deliberate expressiveness and how this boundary has shifted over time.

Explorations of the connection between portamento and legato has also led scholars to question the broader meaning and role of portamento. In particular, several researchers have suggested that there is a connection between portamento and speech; this is an avenue that I also intend to pursue throughout this Element. In situating portamento as an integral part of vocalism, Deborah Kauffman was the first to suggest that portamento might have had the general aim of making singing more reminiscent of speaking.[28] In the final section of John Potter's article about portamento, which analyses recordings by Adelina Patti, Nellie Melba and other opera singers, the author speculates that 'portamento helped give an illusion of language, re-creating the contour (as opposed to the sound) of speech in exaggerated form'.[29] Daniel Leech-Wilkinson, in an article that is more speculative and exploratory than purely empirical, suggests that portamento can be seen as an example of the more 'emotionally straightforward' nature of musical performance before the Second World War,[30] one that appealed to older audiences because it mimicked their earliest, most instinctive emotional responses to musical sounds.[31]

Primary sources suggest that this connection between portamento and language can be productive in the study of performance practice in *zarzuela*, while

---

[25] Morales Villar, *Los tratados de canto en España*, 373.

[26] Rebecca Plack, 'The Substance of Style: How Singing Creates Sound in Lieder Recordings 1902–1939' (PhD thesis, Princeton University, 2008), 19.

[27] Plack, 'The Substance of Style', 44.

[28] Kauffman, 'Portamento in Romantic Opera', 150.

[29] Potter, 'Beggar at the Door', 550.

[30] Daniel Leech-Wilkinson, 'Portamento and Musical Meaning', *Journal of Musicological Research* 25, nos. 3/4 (2006): 233–261, especially 258.

[31] Leech-Wilkinson, 'Portamento and Musical Meaning', 248.

at the same time illuminating features unique to *zarzuela* that are not present in other genres. As discussed above, written primary sources are not always terribly helpful in clarifying the attributes of a good *zarzuela* performance (as opposed to opera) and likewise the overarching principles that governed the use of portamento. The singing treatises that were in use at the conservatoires and in private singing studios throughout the period 1850–1950 often point out that portamento should be used with discernment and good taste, but without explaining in detail what this actually meant. This aligns with singing treatises elsewhere in Europe, as discussed above.[32] These treatises are also not specific to *zarzuela* and so they do not offer hints as to what makes a good performance in this particular genre.

Reviews published in newspapers also tend to provide little detail about specific aspects of performance. Singers' performances were usually described with just a few words or, at best, a couple of sentences. General adjectives (e.g., '*graciosa*' (graceful)) were used to tell about the performer, without any detailed discussions of specific stylistic elements. Specialized music periodicals often provided more detailed commentary, but writers here tended to focus on matters of composition and the troubled relationship between *zarzuela* and Spanish opera or on general news and gossip about musical life and *zarzuela* companies.

There is, however, a constant that runs throughout the *zarzuela*-focused musical press and music criticism that can provide a guiding principle to evaluate portamento (and other performance elements) in historical recordings: namely, the idea that good singing in *zarzuela* equated good, expressive and communicative singing in the Spanish language. In reviews of *zarzuela* performances, '*decir*' (to say) was often used interchangeably with '*cantar*' (to sing), with reviewers frequently praising *zarzuela* singers for *saying* their role very well.[33] This focus on text can be connected to the concept of *naturalidad* or *naturalismo* (naturalness, spontaneity), which reviewers often invoked as a desirable quality in *zarzuela* performance, usually in opposition to what was heard as artificiality and affectation in other genres, such as opera.[34] The requirement to convey text expressively in singing was also linked to the expectation that *zarzuela* performers should be convincing when reciting and acting during the sections of

---

[32] Morales Villar, *Los tratados de canto en España*, 373 and 454.

[33] For example, R. Blasco, 'Parish', *La correspondencia de España*, 3 October 1897, and A. [full name unknown], 'En el teatro de la ópera', *El País*, 13 December 1895.

[34] Un vecino de Madrid [pseudonym], 'Chicos y grandes', *Juan Rana*, 26 November 1897; 'Teatro de Parish', *El globo*, 23 October 1899; 'Marina en el Tívoli', *Heraldo Nacional*, 17 October 1915; 'Teatros', *Diario oficial de avisos de Madrid*, 25 January 1891; 'Teatro de la Zarzuela', *El día*, 4 February 1894.

spoken dialogue (which, as will be discussed later, were not included in recordings). *Zarzuela* singers were therefore expected to communicate Spanish-language text expressively and in different ways throughout a performance: to sing *zarzuela* well was often equated with being able to sing well in Spanish.

Within *zarzuela* circles, these factors contributed to defining the genre's expressive codes and how audiences received them. Their manifestations in *zarzuela* were seen as being somewhat distinct from those of opera, while still sharing significant common ground. In the early decades of *zarzuela* development, pioneers such as Francisco Asenjo Barbieri repeatedly complained that the professors at the conservatoire, as well as others teaching privately in Spain, did not teach their students to sing in Spanish (vocal training at the time was focused mostly or solely on Italian-language materials). Musicologist Antonio Cotarelo y Mori notes that some singers, in order to be able to sing *zarzuela*, had to retrain after completing their degrees at the conservatoire, although he did not explain where or with whom they did this.[35] Composer Emilio Arrieta, who directed the Escuela Nacional de Música y Declamación from 1868, was credited with providing increased performance opportunities for students of singing,[36] but advocates of Spanish opera still claimed that students were not learning to sing properly in Spanish.[37] This further suggests that *zarzuela* composers and supporters acknowledged that singing in Spanish necessitated approaches and techniques that were at least in some respects different from those required to sing Italian opera, even though details of such approaches and techniques were not explicitly explained.

It is the recordings themselves which can therefore offer some starting points in terms of understanding how the principle of communicating a text expressively might have been realized in performance. In fact, even a cursory listen to a few recordings quickly reveals that the ability to sing in Spanish did not necessarily equate with text intelligibility. While this might have to do with technical limitations (especially in the case of earlier recordings), what the body of recordings suggests overall is that intelligibility was not a gold standard and that a performance could preserve some of the text's expressiveness even if not every word was clearly understandable.

---

[35] Cotarelo y Mori, *Historia de la zarzuela*, 538–539.

[36] Escuela Nacional de Música y Declamación, *La correspondencia de España*, 23 February 1881.

[37] Celsa Alonso, 'Ruperto Chapí: Música, pragmatismo y heterodoxia', in Víctor Sánchez Sánchez, Javier Suárez Pajares and Vicente Galbis López, eds., *Ruperto Chapí: Nuevas perspectivas* (Valencia: Institut Valencià de la Música, 2012), 23–51, especially 37.

One such example is Pilar Duamirg's recording of the well-known aria 'Pensar en él' from *Marina*, recorded for Parlophon in 1930.[38] Duamirg's pronunciation is almost unintelligible; however, she conveys a strong sense of spoken speech. She subtly manipulates note values, shortening some and lengthening others, in order to adapt her singing to the cadences of spoken Spanish. Duamirg introduces localized rubato in key places to achieve the same effect. Central to this study, she employs portamento to emphasize key moments in the text and to highlight some of her tempo modifications. This performance, while musically interesting on its own, is better understood within the context of several decades of changing conventions regarding portamento and how it was documented in recordings, the focus of this Element.

Zarzuela on Wax Cylinders, 1896–1905

The first recordings ever made of *zarzuela* are likely lost forever. These took place during public demonstrations of the newly invented phonograph that took place in Spain between 1878 and 1882 and then more frequently throughout the early to mid 1890s.[39] At that time, sound recording technologies had not yet developed into machines intended for domestic use. Instead, Spaniards would gather in theatres, cafes, clubs, churches or larger private homes – or visit commercial premises (*salones fonográficos*) – to watch an operator demonstrate the phonograph. The main purpose of these demonstration sessions was for audiences to be reassured first hand that the phonograph was indeed capable of recording and playing back sound. It is likely that the resulting recordings were discarded quickly after the demonstration, with little if any thought given to their preservation.

To show off the phonograph's capabilities, the operator would normally choose a range of sounds with which audiences would be familiar, such as military calls, animal sounds, jokes and short speeches, opera arias, traditional songs and, indeed, *zarzuela* romanzas. On some occasions, some of these would be recorded in front of the audience by local singers or speakers and then immediately played back, a process which reassured those present that the

---

[38] Pilar Duamirg, 'Pensar en él Rondó', by Emilio Arrieta, recorded ca. 1930 for Parlophon, matrix no. 71051. A publicly available digitized version or modern reissue is not available; the recording was accessed through an on-demand digitization, for research purposes only, made by the Biblioteca Nacional de España.

[39] The first series of demonstrations (1878–1882) took place after the phonograph was first invented. Interest in demonstrations faded soon thereafter. When Edison launched his Perfected Phonograph in 1888, interest resumed. See Eva Moreda Rodríguez, *Inventing the Recording: The Phonograph and National Culture in Spain, 1877–1914* (New York: Oxford University Press, 2021), 17–62.

operator had not manipulated or faked the recording in any way.[40] Press reviews typically speak of the audience's wonderment at the phonograph's capabilities, but they tend to provide little or no detail on the titles of the *zarzuela* numbers that were recorded, who sang them and whether the singers changed their performance in any way when recording.

There are a few exceptions, such as the press notices for a private *salón fonográfico* that a Mr Pertierra kept open in Madrid in 1894 and 1895. From advertisements, we know that Pertierra's *zarzuela* repertoire included selections from recent works such as *El gorro frigio* (1893), *Certamen nacional* (1888) and *La verbena de la Paloma* (1894) sung by well-known performers active on the Madrid stages, namely Emilio Mesejo, Joaquina Pino, Loreto Prado and Lucrecia Arana.[41] It is remarkable that Pertierra managed to secure some of the most successful and best-known performers of the time, since, as will be discussed later, in the early years of commercial recording it was more common for companies to employ rank and file, lesser-known singers. Mesejo, in particular, never recorded in the era of commercial phonography and Arana only did so in a sustained way during the final years of her career.[42] The lack of surviving pre-commercial cylinders means that we might be missing out on potentially important sources that would allow us to obtain a fuller picture about *zarzuela* performance practices in the 1890s (and even earlier), since the careers of some of these singers went back to the 1870s or even the 1860s.

The official arrival of commercial phonography in Spain can be dated to December 1896, with the opening in Madrid of the first *gabinete fonográfico*, Hugens y Acosta. *Gabinetes* were small establishments – often operating as a sideline to an established business, such as a pharmacy or an optician's office – that imported phonographs to sell to the public. They also recorded their own wax cylinders, using Edison machines, with local singers and instrumentalists. The *gabinetes* era was short-lived. Hugens y Acosta, which was also the last of them to close, did so in 1905. They were unable to face competition from the international firm of Gramophone Company, Ltd., which Emile Berliner founded in London in 1898. During these nine years, about forty *gabinetes*

---

[40] *El fonógrafo en el teatro*, *La Rioja*, 24 June 1894; *Espectáculo científico*, *La correspondencia de España*, 27 June 1894; *Espectáculos*, *La correspondencia de España*, 26 December 1894.

[41] *Notable fonógrafo*, *El popular*, 23 May 1894; *Noticias*, *La Unión Católica*, 25 May 1894; *Espectáculo científico*, *La correspondencia de España*, 27 June 1894; *Fonógrafo*, *La Iberia*, 10 January 1895; *Noticias*, *La correspondencia de España*, 3 February 1895; *Madrid*, *El Correo Militar*, 11 February 1895; *Noticias*, *El correo militar*, 9 March 1895; *Noticias*, *El día*, 18 March 1895.

[42] Arana retired in 1908 and her first recordings for Gramophone are from 1904. She did record before that for small Spanish labels, but the fact that only one of her cylinders survives (at Eresbil) suggests that she did not do so prolifically.

operated for various lengths of time in several cities and towns across Spain, but most were in Madrid, Barcelona and Valencia.[43]

The number of surviving cylinders from the *gabinetes* currently held in public collections now amounts to about 1300 and about 300 of these are of *zarzuelas*. While this seemingly small number appears to constitute only a small part of the total output of the *gabinetes*, recording *zarzuela* actually constituted a sizeable part of the activities of these firms. *Zarzuela* was actually the third most represented genre among these cylinders, after brass band music – recordings of which might have been so plentiful not necessarily because of the genre's popularity but because it was technologically easier to record than other genres – and opera.[44] There is also evidence that *zarzuela* was being recorded outside Spain in these early years, notably by Pathé Frères in France. Pathé cylinders were not playable on Edison machines and vice versa, so the circulation of Pathé recordings and devices might have been somewhat limited during these years in Spain. Only one Spanish collection of Pathé cylinders containing *zarzuela* examples is known to survive.[45]

The reasons why *zarzuela* was one of the first genres to be extensively recorded in Spain are easy to understand. The genre was extremely popular with audiences, especially in the cities, most notably Madrid. The subgenre known as *género chico* in particular had evolved into a veritable mass entertainment industry. To understand the popularity of *género chico*, we need to go back to the birth of *zarzuela* in its modern form in the mid nineteenth century.[46]

At this time, the predominant *zarzuela* format was *zarzuela grande*, as introduced by Francisco Asenjo Barbieri in *Jugar con fuego* (1851). It consisted of three acts and featured a range of musical numbers linked by spoken dialogue. *Zarzuela grande* drew upon European models such as Italian *bel canto* and French *opéra comique* and infused these approaches with Spanish traditional and historical dance rhythms as well as with Spanish settings and stories to create something distinctively Spanish. *Zarzuela grande* was at first

---

[43] Moreda Rodríguez, *Inventing the Recording*, 64–123.

[44] Eva Moreda Rodríguez, 'Recording *zarzuela grande* in Spain in the Early Days of the Phonograph and Gramophone', in Samuel Llano, Matthew Machin-Autenrieth and Salwa Castelo-Branco, eds., *Music, Nation and Region in the Iberian Peninsula* (Champaign, IL: University of Illinois Press, 2023), 83–99, at 87–90.

[45] This is the Colección Imprenta Pérez, which belonged to Leandro Pérez, a printmaker from Huesca in the north of Aragón. It contains about a dozen *zarzuela* items out of approximately 230 cylinders. Digitizations of the collection can be accessed through the Documentos y Archivos de Aragón (Archives and Documents from Aragon) website: https://dara.aragon.es/opac/app/results/?st=.3.563202.564567.

[46] While a musical-theatrical genre called *zarzuela* existed in Baroque Spain until the mid eighteenth century, the beginnings of modern *zarzuela* are typically dated to 1849, with the premiere of Rafael Hernando's *Colegialas y soldados*.

remarkably popular with middle class audiences in Madrid and elsewhere, but from the mid 1860s, new works were failing to gain the accolades of their predecessors, a situation that put the future of the genre at risk.[47]

A lasting solution to the crisis came through the *teatro por horas* format. Madrid audiences had been becoming increasingly enthralled with *teatro por horas* (literally, theatre by the hour) since 1868,[48] when theatre impresarios replaced their customary full length spoken plays, which typically lasted three to four hours, with four one-hour plays. Performances started in the late evening and continued until midnight.[49] Tickets for each play were sold separately, which increased profits for impresarios and minimized risk since unsuccessful or unpopular plays could be easily replaced. While *teatro por horas* was initially used only for spoken plays, *zarzuela* producers also eventually adopted the format. The shorter, one-act *zarzuelas* started to be collectively known as *género chico* (literally, the small genre), with Federico Chueca's *La canción de la Lola* (1880) generally being acknowledged as the first work in the new format.

Apart from being shorter to fit the parameters of *teatro por horas*, *género chico* works were different from *zarzuela grande* in ways that could sometimes demand different approaches to performance. The subject matter of *género chico* works was comic and lighter than those of *zarzuela grande*; plots and characters were subjected to a higher degree of standardization, as suited the commercial nature of the new subgenre. Furthermore, the music started to show greater influences from Spanish traditional and popular genres (as opposed to Italian *bel canto*) and strophic songs became more frequent. The latter facilitated memorization in a context where actors were forced to learn new material quickly, since the same music was sung to different words. Like *zarzuela grande*, *género chico* still used predominantly Spanish settings and themes, but now the *pueblo* was placed firmly at its centre. This meant that it focused on the Spanish working and lower middle classes, including peasants, skilled and unskilled urban workers, artisans, small business owners such as shopkeepers and, in some cases, lowlife characters. The genre's portrayal of the *pueblo* was designed to be palatable and appealing to the bourgeoisie, the upper classes and

---

[47] See Enrique Mejías García, 'La correspondencia de los bufos (1871): Ideología de un teatro musical divertido en una España en transformación', *Revista de Musicología*, 31, no. 1 (2008): 125–149, especially 127–133.

[48] Interestingly, Deleito y Piñuela highlights the fact that 1868 was also the year of the Glorious Revolution, which resulted in the deposition of Queen Isabella II, in an attempt to intimately connect the history of the *género chico* with key political events in Spanish history. See José Deleito y Piñuela, *Origen y apogeo del género chico* (Madrid: Revista de Occidente, 1949), 1.

[49] Rafael Gil Osorio y Sánchez, 'Los teatros de hora', *La correspondencia de España*, 6 July 1881, 3–4.

the aristocracy,[50] while at the same time allowing the working and lower middle classes to recognize themselves in the characters.[51] As a result, the class dimension of *zarzuela* audiences expanded with respect to what had been the norm earlier.

As *género chico* developed, longer-format *zarzuelas* were still being performed and written (e.g., Ruperto Chapí's *La tempestad* (1882) and *El rey que rabió* (1891), both of which were immensely popular), although their appeal remained more limited to the middle and upper classes.[52] Even though in the late nineteenth century separate companies and theatres existed for *género chico, zarzuela grande* and opera[53] and *zarzuela grande* performers were expected to have received operatic training in ways that *género chico* performers were not, an examination of the career patterns of individual singers shows that some noted *género chico* performers, such as Lucrecia Arana, did indeed have operatic training[54] and that, all in all, the genres were relatively permeable. *Zarzuela* singers moved not only between *zarzuela* and opera but also between *zarzuela grande* and *género chico* as well as between *zarzuela*, lighter forms of entertainment and spoken theatre. Decisions to move between genres depended on one's vocal and acting ability (which changed with age) and also on the perceived prestige of different styles, financial considerations, available opportunities and personal preference.[55]

It was against this backdrop that the *gabinetes fonográficos* were first established and started recording *zarzuela* as a vibrant and lively stage genre. The *gabinetes* had to contend with a number of limitations and challenges (technological, commercial, cultural and sociological) that considerably shaped what they could offer and what we can hear in their recordings nowadays. Some of these limitations, challenges and particularities are common to the global recording industry at this point in time, while others are more specific to Spain. First, the *gabinetes* did not put dates on their cylinders and catalogues were scarce, so attempting to draw firm conclusions regarding how styles might have evolved between the last years of the nineteenth century and the early years

---

[50] Clinton D. Young, *Music Theater and Popular Nationalism in Spain, 1880–1930* (Baton Rouge, LA: Louisiana State University Press, 2016), 35; Carmen del Moral Ruiz, *El género chico: Ocio y teatro en Madrid (1880–1910)* (Madrid: Alianza, 2004), 154; Nancy J. Membrez, *The* Teatro Por Horas: *History, Dynamics and Comprehensive Bibliography of a Madrid Industry, 1867–1922* (PhD dissertation, University of Michigan, 1987), 115–116; Zeda [pseudonym], 'Crónica general', *El teatro*, 48 (1904), 1–2.

[51] Del Moral Ruiz, *El género chico*, 154.

[52] Blasco, 'Parish', 2.

[53] Companies moved between theatres. In Madrid, for example, a company's tenure in a theatre lasted for around nine months, starting around September and ending in June.

[54] Rodríguez Arnáez, *Lucrecia Arana: Jarrera castiza*, 22.

[55] 'Isidro Soler', *El arte del teatro*, 58 (1908), 9–11; Miquis, 'Bohemios', *El teatro*, 43 (1904), 13; 'Balbina Valverde', *El teatro*, 11 (1901), 11–12.

of the twentieth is problematic.[56] Second, recordings made by the *gabinetes fonográficos* were almost always unique. Due to technological limitations, duplication was generally only possible by means of a pantograph, which meant that resulting copies were limited in number and of poor quality. Many of the most active Spanish *gabinetes* took pride in the fact that their products were one-of-a-kind and individually crafted, rather than mass-produced.[57] For matters of performance practice, this has significant implications in that *gabinetes* and singers were likely more concerned with ensuring that each of their recordings was good enough to be sold rather than with producing a perfect version of any given piece. Importantly, these recordings therefore preserve some of the spontaneous, 'in the moment' quality of live performance.[58]

Additionally, the *gabinetes* faced the challenge of making their customers accept the new medium of recording as a faithful representation of reality. This was a challenge that Spanish recordists shared with others elsewhere in the world, but the situation in Spain had some particular characteristics. Familiarity was key: *gabinetes* did not try to introduce their audiences to new repertoires, but rather focused on music which buyers would know well, be it older, established works or the latest hits. But the genre's ever-evolving, multimedia practices were not easy to capture on record, particularly on two-minute cylinders.[59] *Zarzuela*, particularly *género chico*, was a robust industry in which the act of seeing any stage performance would have been significantly coloured by the experience of seeing similar works live on stage on a regular basis, perhaps even daily.[60] The *gabinetes* certainly made some attempts to capitalize on live performances. A majority of the *gabinetes* in Madrid, for example, were located near the *género chico* theatres, where they could have attracted theatre-goers as customers and also have ready access to singers.[61]

---

[56] Other information, such as the premiere dates for *zarzuelas* and singers' career information, can be used to approximate the dating of some cylinders; however, there is no firm evidence to date any one cylinder conclusively in 1896. See Moreda Rodríguez, *Inventing the Recording*, 127–128.

[57] Moreda Rodríguez, *Inventing the Recording*, 69–70.

[58] This point is also supported by the analysis of other elements of performances such as cadenzas. In recordings of the same aria by the same performer, cadenzas are not normally repeated *verbatim*, though they typically showed significant similarities. This suggests that the performer would have a pool of gestures and devices to choose from, which they would then put together in different ways for each performance – and in each recording session. See Eva Moreda Rodríguez, 'Amateur Recording on the Phonograph in *fin-de-siècle* Barcelona: Practices, Repertoires and Performers in the Regordosa-Turull Wax Cylinder Collection', *Journal of the Royal Musical Association* 145, no. 2 (2020): 385–415, especially 409–411.

[59] *Gabinetes* used two-minute cylinders (as opposed to four-minute ones, introduced at a later stage). By reducing the rotation speed, the cylinders' time could be extended to about 2:30–2:45 minutes.

[60] Del Moral Ruiz, *El género chico*, 21.

[61] Moreda Rodríguez, *Inventing the Recording*, 97.

The gabinetes were also forced to make adaptations that quickly became widely accepted conventions in the nascent recording industry. Two of these are of particular importance. First, the limited duration of cylinders made it impossible to seamlessly record a full *zarzuela* and even individual numbers had sometimes had to be shortened through cuts (rather than through faster speeds).[62] Second, spoken dialogue was not recorded; only the musical numbers were.

Even though it would have been possible for *gabinetes* to split a long number across two (or more) cylinders, examples of this practice are very rare, which suggests that the illusion of seamless performance was, from early on, important to early recordists and listeners. There is no evidence, moreover, that recordists were at this stage thinking beyond individual numbers: *gabinetes* were not producing 'full' *zarzuela* or opera recordings by selling several numbers of the same work together (perhaps, at least in part, because of the high costs this would have incurred) and similarly singers did not have the opportunity at this stage to construct a full-length performance on record (as they would later on).

Although spoken dialogue was regarded as an important part of the genre in *zarzuela* circles (with performers being expected to recite dialogue convincingly), dialogue never made it onto *zarzuela* recordings, other than quick interjections in the middle of a number. These typically occurred in *zarzuelas* set in urban, working class environments such as *Agua, azucarillos y aguardiente* and *La verbena de la Paloma*. The question as to why dialogue was systematically cut does not have a straightforward answer. The *gabinetes* also sold spoken word recordings that featured comedy routines, short stories or speeches (as did other manufacturers of cylinders). These were sold at lower prices than music cylinders and were eventually discontinued, which implies that they were not very popular with audiences. However, in the same way that the *gabinetes* experimented with spoken word cylinders, they could also have experimented with *zarzuela* dialogue, though there is no evidence to suggest that they did so. In contemporary opera recordings from around the world, recitative was also commonly left out, so it is plausible that *gabinetes* simply took their cue from elsewhere and adopted the practice to their own conventions.

Despite the *gabinetes*' significant technological and cultural breakthroughs, their impact on broader society remained limited at the time and it should not be assumed that music listening practices were transformed in any meaningful way. In particular, the *zarzuela* theatre industry remained relatively impervious to new technological developments, with the obvious exceptions of the singers

---

[62] For example, a *zarzuela grande* duet or trio could be turned into a romanza by removing one or two longer phrases from one of the roles.

who recorded them. Theatre and *zarzuela* publications of the time, such as the magazines *Juan Rana* and *El arte del teatro*, only mention the phonograph and mostly under the guise of general commentary or satire rather than offering considered commentary of individual recordings. Composers at the time concerned themselves more with protecting their intellectual rights in order to secure financial benefits from live performances than engaging with the recording industry. Since the *gabinetes* were only a small industry, it seems likely that composers did not see many financial advantages in working with them.

These considerations notwithstanding, a significant number of the surviving wax cylinders reflect high levels of vocal technique and artistic quality. One example is Eloísa López-Marán's recording of 'Brindis' from Manuel Fernández Caballero's popular *zarzuela La viejecita* (1897).[63] This performance illustrates how portamento might have been used at the time, in combination with other performing decisions, to create an expressive performance that attempted to somehow mimic the shape of the text and convey an impression of spoken speech.

A dozen cylinders by López-Marán survive, making her one of the early *zarzuela* performers for whom we have the most recordings. This quantity suggests that she recorded extensively, even though her stage career was not particularly illustrious. López-Marán studied with the then-famed teacher Napoleón Verger, but notices about her stage career are limited to a handful of reviews for performances in Madrid opera and *zarzuela* theatres between 1894 and 1901.[64] She was typical of most singers who recorded for the *gabinetes* in that she was not a star performer. (This is consistent with practices elsewhere.) The recording industry at this point was considered too much of an uncertainty to attract sustained interest from major singers. Surviving recordings as well as catalogues from *gabinetes* suggest that companies might have relied to a considerable extent on a relatively small number of vocalists who recorded prolifically[65] and who likely stood out for their ability to quickly adapt to recording technologies and the recording studio.

López-Marán, in her recording of 'Brindis', suggests that she was one of these singers (see Figure 1). At the start of the passage, the tempo moves steadily (bars 1–7), and the portamentos are discreet (in bars 3 and 5), more

---

[63] Eloísa Lopez-Marán (as señorita Marán), 'Brindis', by Manuel Fernández-Caballero, recorded ca. 1900 for Álvaro Ureña, no matrix or catalogue number, http://bdh.bne.es/bnesearch/detalle/bdh0000046536, from 0:10.

[64] Anonymous, 'Noticias de espectáculos', *El día*, 14 June 1894; Anonymous, 'Parish', *Revista contemporánea* 109 (1898), 335; A. [full name unknown], 'Parish', *La ilustración española e hispanoamericana*, 8 February 1898; 'Teatro de Parish', *La Iberia*, 6 February 1898; 'Teatro del Buen Retiro', *El globo*, 9 June 1898.

[65] Moreda Rodríguez, *Inventing the Recording*, 135.

Figure 1 Bars 5 to 20 from 'Brindis', from Manuel Fernández Caballero's *La viejecita*. Portamento and fermatas have been added in grey to reflect Eloísa López-Marán's performance

akin to a well-sustained legato that López-Marán might have used to efficiently prolong the vocal line than to achieve a deliberate vocal effect. The next portamento (bar 7) is obviously more deliberate: clear and well-controlled, it moves from the fermata down to the leading tone, in what amounts to a very commonplace use of portamento in recordings of *zarzuela* from these and later days. The dotted quavers soon thereafter might have invited further discreet portamentos (bar 11), but López-Marán chose not to do so and therefore isolated the word 'ingratos' (ungrateful) from the rest of the line in an obvious dramatic effect. A few bars later, the portamentos are again prominent (bars 14–15), along with small-scale decelerations of the tempo. When combined, these performance choices provide a sense of closure to the section while building up expectations for the next one. We could have expected a portamento on the word 'ellos' (bar 15), as portamento was also exceedingly common in descending fourths, but López-Marán again decided otherwise. At the same time she chose not to slow down any further, perhaps to avoid a sense of exaggerated deceleration.

    López-Marán's performance of this passage reveals some underlying principles concerning the use of portamento that recur in several of these earlier (and also later) recordings. Portamento is often combined with tempo decelerations so that the singer can emphasize not so much a specific word but rather a part of a sentence, thereby giving dramatic shape to the line. Remarkably, *La viejecita* is a *género chico* work, which in principle might have been thought of as less receptive to elements of operatic performance like portamento. López-Marán's recording, however, confirms that portamento could indeed be used liberally and intelligently within the subgenre.

There are a limited number of *zarzuela* romanzas for which more than one cylinder survives (typically no more than three or four). These are generally from works that enjoyed successful premieres during the time of the *gabinetes*. Such is the case with both *La viejecita* and Fernández Caballero's other hit, *Gigantes y cabezudos* (1898). The plot of *Gigantes y cabezudos* referred to the then-current Spanish-American war over Cuba. The *zarzuela* became a success in large part because of how it depicted the ambivalent attitude of many Spaniards towards the war, which was largely seen as a heroic yet vain effort that came at an enormous cost to Spanish society. Comparing these recordings can provide us with a glimpse into the general parameters that governed the use of portamento and how a performer might have chosen to use portamento in a specific performance following these guidelines. At the same time they preserve some of the spontaneity and live quality of recordings at the time. Illustrative examples are cylinders of 'Esta es su carta' from *Gigantes y cabezudos* as recorded by Adela Taberner[66] and by Marina Gurina[67] (see Figures 2a and 2b) and 'Canción del espejo' from *La viejecita* by Blanca del Carmen[68] and by Pepita Alcácer[69] (see Figures 3a and 3b).

Such recordings allow us to observe some of the tacit rules that governed the use of portamento. First, descending portamentos were more common than ascending ones, although the latter definitely existed. The appearance of ascending portamentos actually contradicts one of the very few specific instructions about portamento found in singing treatises such as *El cant (llibre per al cantat i per l'aficionat)*, written several decades later by the celebrated tenor Emili Vendrell, who said that ascending portamento was 'anti-artistic and in bad taste'.[70] Second, portamento

---

[66] Adela Taberner, 'Esta es su carta', by Manuel Fernández-Caballero, recorded ca. 1900 for Centro Fonográfico Manuel Moreno Casas, no matrix or catalogue number, http://bdh.bne.es/bnesearch/detalle/bdh0000046154.

[67] Marina Gurina, 'Esta es su carta', by Manuel Fernández Caballero, recorded privately ca. 1900 by Ruperto Regordosa, no matrix or catalogue number, https://mdc.csuc.cat/digital/collection/sonorbc/id/75/rec/17.

[68] Blanca Del Carmen, 'Canción del espejo', by Manuel Fernández Caballero', recorded ca. 1900 for Viuda de Aramburo, no matrix or catalogue number, http://bdh.bne.es/bnesearch/detalle/bdh0000046527.

[69] Pepita Alcácer, 'Canción del espejo', by Manuel Fernández Caballero, recorded ca. 1900 privately by Ruperto Regordosa, https://mdc.csuc.cat/digital/collection/sonorbc/id/71/rec/2.

[70] Emili Vendrell, *El cant (llibre per al cantat u per l'aficionat)* (Barcelona: Sucesor de E. Meseguer, 1955), 142.

Figure 2a and 2b Bars 40–51 from the *Tiempo de vals lento* 'Esta es su carta', from Manuel Fernández Caballero's *Gigantes y cabezudos*, with portamento added as performed by Adela Taberner and Marina Gurina respectively

Figure 3a and 3b Bars 4–11 from 'Cancion del espejo', from Manuel Fernández Caballero's *La viejecita*, with portamento added as performed by Blanca del Carmen and Pepita Alcácer

tended to be used for intervals of a fourth or larger, rather than for smaller ones. For smaller intervals, when portamento does appear, it tends to take the form of an exaggerated legato, as in the López-Marán recording (see Figure 1). This approach becomes more prominent in later recordings, as we will see. Third, portamento tended to appear more at the ends of phrases than at the beginnings.

The approaches to musicianship displayed in the recordings by López-Marán, Del Carmen, Taberner, Gurina and Alcácer at first might sound unusual because of the portamentos and tempo fluctuations, which become increasingly apparent after several sessions of attentive, unprejudiced listening. Some performers used portamento more profusely and others more sparingly, but in every case it eventually becomes possible to recognize the expressive intentions achieved through portamento.

Other *gabinete* recordings, however, might be more difficult to interpret in expressive and musical terms. This comes as a useful reminder of two important considerations: 1) the need to disentangle what we hear in early recordings in terms of performance practice and 2) the multifaceted, hybrid nature of *zarzuela*. Both aspects are central to this Element and therefore deserve further exploration.

To illuminate the first point, I will focus on a recording of 'Salve' from *Gigantes y cabezudos*, the final number of the *zarzuela*, performed by an unnamed chorus at the Corrons *gabinete* in Barcelona. Choral recordings are relatively rare within the earlier *zarzuela* recording output (as is typical of the earlier phonograph era). The chorus often appears at pivotal moments in many *zarzuelas*, including *Gigantes y cabezudos*. Here, it represents the people of the *pueblo*, who either come together and sing of their identity or express patriotic feelings, the latter more often than not with a hint of humor and irony. Recording even a small group of singers multiplied the difficulties of recording a single soloist.[71] Some *gabinetes* and private recordists eventually developed acceptable solutions to record *zarzuela* choirs in what was likely a highly experimental process,[72] but the number of such recordings remained small.[73]

In the 'Salve' recording, portamento is employed on nearly every descending fourth and fifth interval; this is particularly evident at the end of phrases. By

---

[71] The choirs in *gabinetes* recordings are often uncredited, as in the Corrons recording, which suggests that the ensemble was put together *ad hoc* in the recording room. Sometimes, though, the chorus of a specific theatre is credited, although it is likely that it was not the full choir that was recorded, but rather a select number of singers.

[72] See Moreda Rodríguez, 'Amateur Recording on the Phonograph in *fin-de-siècle* Barcelona', 405–406, and the same author's 'Reconstructing Zarzuela Performance Practices ca. 1900: Wax Cylinder and Gramophone Disc Recordings of *Gigantes y cabezudos*', *Journal of Musicology*, 37, no. 4 (2020): 459–487, especially 474–475.

[73] Recordings of choirs in genres other than *zarzuela* (e.g., opera, traditional music) are even rarer in Spain.

contrast, when considering the small number of other choral recordings from the time, portamento is either used sparingly or not at all.[74] When recording a soloist, the decision to use or not use portamento could have been made on the spot. It is less likely that this was the case when it came to ensembles, which would require some rehearsal in their collective use of portamento. In the portamento-rich 'Salve', the use of portamento is so pronounced that the performance risks becoming unmusical. This suggests that the use of portamento was a very deliberate decision and that the choice was perhaps not so much musical as it was technical. Portamento, indeed, could have functioned here as a kind of extended legato that helped the choir keep a semblance of vocal line while singing together and was something with which they experimented in the recording room in order to alleviate the problems inherent in recording even small choirs.

Such a hypothesis opens up the possibility that performers – especially those who were more experienced making recordings or those who had worked under the direction of a knowledgeable recordist – consciously adapted their performing styles to suit the phonograph. With their awareness that some dimensions of the sound could not and would not be captured, they instead tried to compensate or replace those aspects with others. I have suggested elsewhere that the briskness of the tempo in some of these earlier recordings might have been another result of these conditions[75] and similar conclusions concerning such compensatory mechanisms have been advanced in recent empirical studies involving modern performers recording on early-style phonographs.[76]

Another example of an outlier recording is that of 'Canción de Paloma' from Francisco Asenjo Barbieri's classic *zarzuela El barberillo de Lavapiés* (1874) by an unnamed singer for Pathé, the budding French multinational that also occasionally recorded *zarzuela* in these years. This recording, therefore, offers a rare example of an early *zarzuela* recording made outside Spain.[77] As such, it provides a broader context for the practices developed by early Spanish

---

[74] Artistas del Teatro Apolo, 'Por fin te miro, Ebro famoso', by Manuel Fernández Caballero, recorded ca. 1900 for La fonográfica madrileña, no matrix or catalogue number, http://bdh.bne .es/bnesearch/detalle/bdh0000046363; Coro del Teatro de la Zarzuela, 'Por fin te miro, Ebro famoso', by Manuel Fernández Caballero, recorded ca. 1900 for Hugens y Acosta, no matrix or catalogue number, http://bdh.bne.es/bnesearch/detalle/bdh0000046425; Coro de la Gran Vía, 'Tango', by Gerónimo Giménez, recorded ca. 1900 for Centro Fonográfico Moreno Casas, no matrix or catalogue number, http://bdh.bne.es/bnesearch/detalle/bdh0000046307.

[75] Moreda Rodríguez, 'Reconstructing *Zarzuela* Performance Practices', 475.

[76] Inja Stanović and Adam Stanović, 'A Chip Off the Old Block? Introducing the Practice of Historically-Informed Recording', *Seismograph* (no issue number) (2021), https://seismograf .org/node/19479.

[77] Unnamed female singer, 'Canción de Paloma', by Francisco Asenjo Barbieri, recorded ca. 1902, Pathé, matrix number 85130 (9002), http://bdh.bne.es/bnesearch/detalle/bdh0000046313, especially ca. 0:54 and 1:13.

recordists and singers in manipulating and interacting with technology. The execution of portamento in this recording might seem disappointing, even when considering the limitations of technology. Sometimes initial and/or final notes are noticeably out of tune, which could reveal a lack of technical control on the part of the singer. We cannot know for sure, however, whether these types of portamentos would have been heard as acceptable by *zarzuela* audiences, but we can contextualize the singer's portamento technique alongside various other performance aspects of the recording. Elsewhere in the romanza, the acciaccaturas are not particularly well executed and musical accents are often misplaced. It is entirely plausible that this recording was not particularly representative of what a good performance would have sounded like on stage. We know that wax cylinder recordings often featured lesser-known singers, some of whom may have been mediocre or inexperienced. We also know that some singers became anxious and struggled when first going into the recording room.[78] Nervousness and an inability to keep a steady airflow might well be the root of a number of the issues described above. Singers on Pathé *zarzuela* recordings are often unnamed, which reveals a certain lack of care in recording the genre. This contrasts greatly with the close attention to detail among some of the *gabinetes*.

The second consideration, the hybrid nature of *zarzuela*, is a key aspect of the genre that in recent years has gained increasing importance in its historiography. Acknowledging *zarzuela*'s hybridity has allowed scholars to reaffirm and strengthen its connections with similar vernacular genres around Europe[79] and this assertion contrasts greatly with earlier writings that insisted on the exceptionality of the genre and which typically dismissed influences from non-Spanish genres, particularly from Italian opera, as contamination.[80] *Zarzuela*, despite being a typically Spanish genre featuring numbers inspired by traditional forms such as *jota* and *guajira*, was by no means isolated from musical developments outside Spain. Influences at different points in the history of *zarzuela* included Italian *bel canto*, French *opéra comique* and *opérette* and German-language operetta, as well as cabaret and other forms of musical theatre, as discussed above.

---

[78] Peres da Costa, *Off the Record*, 14.

[79] Serge Salaün, *Les espectacles en Espagne* (Paris: Presses Sorbonne Nouvelle, 2011), 87–115; Enrique Mejías García, 'Las raíces de la opereta española: Los dos ciegos de Barbieri y Offenbach', in Tobias Brandenberger and Antje Dreyer, eds., *La zarzuela y sus caminos: Del siglo XVII a la actualidad* (Berlin: Lit Verlag, 2016), 97–120; Enrique Mejías García, 'Dinámicas transnacionales en el teatro musical popular: Jacques Offenbach, compositor de zarzuelas (1855–1905)' (PhD thesis, Universidad Complutense de Madrid, 2018).

[80] Such as Cotarelo y Mori, *Historia de la zarzuela*; Antonio Peña y Goñi, *La ópera española y la música dramática en España en el siglo XIX: Apuntes históricos* (Madrid: Instituto Complutense de Ciencias Musicales, 2003) [facsimile of original 1885 edition].

Early recordings prove that hybrid approaches influenced *zarzuela* perform-ance and the use of portamento. For example, in a recording of 'Si las mujeres mandasen' (also from *Gigantes y cabezudos*) made by a señorita Martínez for the Barcelona *gabinete* Corrons,[81] the singer does not use any portamento. This makes her recorded performance highly distinctive from those of Gurina and Taberner in the same role. Martínez's diction comes across as remarkably clear, though her voice does not seem to have the resonance of Taberner's and especially Gurina's.

Martínez's style seems more akin to the popular and traditional styles of singing that focused on clear text enunciation at the expense of vibrato and uniform timbre.[82] In these styles of singing, executing a well-controlled porta-mento will have likely been more difficult. Moreover, it might have been also the case that using portamento in such contexts would have been seen as an affectation that did not align well with the rest of the aesthetic.

Martínez's performance on this recording makes more sense when it is placed within the history of *zarzuela* in the decades preceding the arrival of the phonograph in Spain, as well as within what we know about the singing profession during these years. Although *género chico* preserved the Italian and French influences that had informed earlier *zarzuela*, it also showed an increased capacity to absorb other musical influences and performance genres (e.g., dance, drama).[83] While some singers such as Lucrecia Arana did have operatic training, others simply learned on the job.[84] Press reviews suggest that these performers were stronger actors than singers.[85] Martínez's recording is likely a representative example of this actor-driven approach to performance.

In contrast to Martínez's approach, those of Gurina and López-Marán can likewise be understood within the context of the shifts in vocal technique that were taking place during the late nineteenth century. This was also the time when the idea of vocal registration – the uniformity of timbre across the different registers of the voice – started to impose itself on the operatic world,

---

[81] Señorita Martínez, 'Si las mujeres mandasen', by Manuel Fernández Caballero, recorded for V. Corrons ca. 1900, no matrix or catalogue number, http://bdh.bne.es/bnesearch/detalle/bdh0000046481. A singer by the name of Antonietta Martínez recorded several *zarzuela* numbers for Gramophone in 1899; it is not impossible that this was the same singer, but the gramophone recordings (one of which will be discussed later) reveal a higher vocal range than is heard on the Corrons cylinder.

[82] Eva Moreda Rodríguez, 'Singing and Speaking in Early Twentieth-Century Zarzuela: The Evidence from Early Recordings', *Journal of Musicological Research* 41, no. 1 (2022): 23–49.

[83] Margot Versteeg, *De fusiladores y morcilleros: El discurso cómico del género chico (1870–1910)* (Amsterdam: Brill, 2010), 24–31.

[84] González Peña, Suárez-Pajares and Arce Bueno, *Mujeres de la escena*, 28.

[85] 'Isidro Soler', *El arte del teatro* 58 (1908), 9–11; Miquis, 'Bohemios', *El teatro* 43 (1904), 13; 'Balbina Valverde', *El teatro* 11 (1901), 11–12.

especially as a requirement for singing *verista* roles like those found in the operas of Mascagni and Leoncavallo. This uniformity of timbre was achieved through the raising of the soft palate and the lowering of the larynx, which elongated the vocal tract to maximize resonance and vibrato.[86] Portamento might have been easier to execute for singers familiar with this technique, since register uniformity would have made portamento sound smoother. The vocal tract modifications required to achieve uniformity in register, however, often came at the cost of clear diction.

Hybridity in performing styles, however, did not simply mean that different singers with different vocal techniques and approaches could perform the same roles, as was the case with Pilar in *Gigantes y cabezudos*. It also meant that performers could adapt their own styles to a certain extent by incorporating certain elements (or not), depending on the context. This was the case, for example, with vibrato. While the new operatic vocal techniques discussed above implied that vibrato had to be continuous, in *zarzuela* recordings of this era (and beyond), this is not the case, for it is heard only on certain notes or during specific passages.[87] The same is true of portamento. Choosing whether or not to effect a portamento could mark a certain romanza as being more popular than operatic in nature.

For example, in Emilio Arrieta's *Marina* (first a *zarzuela grande*, then an opera and consistently a popular choice among *gabinetes*),[88] the soprano and tenor romanzas routinely employ portamento,[89] while baritone Roque's *seguidillas* do not.[90] The *seguidillas* offer one example of the sort of numbers inspired by traditional and popular musical forms that proliferated in *zarzuela*, mostly in *género chico* but also in larger scale works such as *Marina*. In their

---

[86] Barbara Gentili, 'The Changing Aesthetics of Vocal Registration in the Age of "Verismo"', *Music and Letters* 102, no. 1 (2020): 54–79, especially 66.

[87] Moreda Rodríguez, 'Singing and Speaking in Early Twentieth-Century *Zarzuela*', 24–25.

[88] *Marina* premiered in 1855 as a *zarzuela*. In 1871, at the request of tenor Enrico Tamberlick, the composer transformed the *zarzuela* into an opera by restructuring the original two acts into three, adding some numbers and expanding the orchestration to reflect that of opera orchestras at the time. See Cortizo, *Emilio Arrieta*, 417 and 423.

[89] Manuel Figuerola, 'Costas las del Levante', by Emilio Arrieta, recorded for Puerto y Novella ca. 1900, no matrix or catalogue number, http://bdh.bne.es/bnesearch/detalle/bdh0000046509; Manuel Guerra, 'No sabes tú', by Emilio Arrieta, recorded for José Navarro ca. 1900, no matrix or catalogue number, http://bdh.bne.es/bnesearch/detalle/bdh0000046422; Rafael Bezares, 'A beber, a beber, a ahogar', by Emilio Arrieta, recorded for Viuda de Aramburo ca. 1900, no matrix or catalogue number, http://bdh.bne.es/bnesearch/detalle/bdh0000046055; unnamed soprano, 'Pensar en él', by Emilio Arrieta, recorded for Viuda de Roselló ca. 1900, no matrix or catalogue number, http://bdh.bne.es/bnesearch/detalle/bdh0000046248.

[90] Juan Reyna, 'Seguidillas', by Emilio Arrieta, recorded for Fono-Reyna ca. 1899, no matrix or catalogue number, http://bdh.bne.es/bnesearch/detalle/bdh0000046434; Señor Marsal, 'Seguidillas', by Emilio Arrieta, recorded for Corrons ca. 1900, no matrix or catalogue number, http://bdh.bne.es/bnesearch/detalle/bdh0000046469.

recordings of *seguidillas*, singers generally limited the use of the expressive devices frequently found in *zarzuela* recordings that were more akin to opera (e.g., ornaments, tempo changes and vibrato) and instead chose fast tempos and vigorous deliveries that seem to show little influence from the more operatic approaches to singing.

In conclusion, while the number of *zarzuela* cylinders that survive is comparatively small and assuming that most of them would have been one-offs, due to the difficulties in the duplication process, the picture that emerges from these scattered examples is as follows. Different approaches to *zarzuela* performance coexisted under the general principle of expressive delivery of text. Portamento often, but not always, became an audible marker that differentiated the operatic approaches from the more popular and vernacular ones.

Zarzuela on 78 rpm Discs, 1899–1924

Between 1899 and 1905, the *gabinetes* coexisted with a newer form of technology that would eventually become dominant and drive them out of business: the gramophone. A key difference between the technologies was that, unlike cylinders, gramophone discs could be duplicated easily and reliably. Gramophone, the London-based manufacturer that was so central to the technology that it took the company's name, developed a strategy that did not need to remain localized, as was the case with the *gabinetes*. Hence, the entire recording industry quickly became more fast-paced and transnational than ever before.

The process was revolutionary. First, Gramophone dispatched scouts around the world. Second, they then either opened branches or absorbed smaller, local labels to establish their foothold in various international markets.[91] These branches allowed Gramophone to record vernacular repertoires while developing various local markets for their products. Czech-language recordings made in Europe, for example, could be sold both in their country of origin and among Czech émigré communities in the USA.[92] Furthermore, a small number of such recordings of vernacular and indigenous repertoires could be marketed to an international audience with an appetite for exotic recordings.[93]

It was during these years that an increased circulation of recordings, including ones of *zarzuela*, began. During the first quarter of the twentieth century, this

---

[91] John R. Bolig, *The Victor Discography: Green, Blue, and Purple Labels (1910–1926)* (Denver: Mainspring Press, 2006), viii–x.

[92] Richard Spottswood, *Ethnic Music on Records: A Discography of Ethnic Recordings Produced in the United States, 1893 to 1942* (Champaign, IL: University of Illinois Press, 1990), vol. 1, xv.

[93] Bolig, *The Victor Discography*, vii.

mobility would result in a more globally cohesive set of musical tastes and listening habits than had previously been the case.[94]

In Spain, this process can be dated back to 1899, the year that Gramophone scouts first visited Madrid and Barcelona. They returned to the same two cities in 1900 and 1902 and in 1903, Gramophone opened a branch in Barcelona. At the time, the *gabinetes* were still operating and many sold Gramophone products alongside their own. It did not take Gramophone long, though, to force the *gabinetes* out of business, with the last one, Hugens y Acosta, closing in 1905, as mentioned in the previous section. Despite rivalries between Gramophone and the *gabinetes*,[95] significant overlaps existed between the two technologies. It is telling, for example, that during their initial visits to Spain, Gramophone signed a significant number of singers who had already recorded for the *gabinetes*. The firm may have approached singers such as Bernardino Blanquer, Ascensión Miralles, Daniel Blanquells, Josefina Huguet, Blanca del Carmen and Manuel Figueroa because of their familiarity with the mechanics of a recording session at a time when few performers understood such things. Or, it is quite possible that these singers might have put themselves forward for the same reason.

Since gramophone discs were still limited in length, recordists and singers did not look beyond individual numbers, following the practice of the *gabinetes*. Many earlier gramophone discs and *gabinete* cylinders, therefore, can be thought of and understood within the same contexts. For example, the internationally successful baritone Marino Aineto recorded the character Roque's 'Seguidillas' from *Marina* for Gramophone in 1902. This was around the same time as the two *gabinetes* recordings discussed in the previous section. While Aineto's voice is obviously attuned to operatic modes of delivery, the three performances can certainly be understood as reflecting the same underlying style and approach to expressiveness with their brisk, regular tempos and sharp diction.[96]

There were, however, key distinctions between gramophone and *gabinete* recordings. First were the differences in technologies and what kinds of sounds recorded better in each format. Second, since Gramophone had access to some of the most prominent opera singers in the world through its international branches, it had little incentive in Spain to record local opera stars and instead focused on *zarzuela*.[97] Third, Gramophone's recording and marketing decisions, by virtue of its global reach, were more complex than had ever been the case with the *gabinetes*.

---

[94] This is the argument developed in Michael Denning, *Noise Uprising: The Audiopolitics of a World Musical Revolution* (London: Verso Books, 2015).

[95] Moreda Rodríguez, *Inventing the Recording*, 85–86.

[96] Marino Aineto, 'Seguidillas', by Emilio Arrieta, recorded for Gramophone in 1902, matrix number 62709, http://bdh.bne.es/bnesearch/detalle/bdh0000179582.

[97] The only Spanish opera singers to make recordings for Gramophone in these early years were those who had international careers in their own right, such as the soprano Josefina Huguet and

Concerning technology, gramophones were said to lack the sensitivity and artisanal nature of phonograph recordings, a fact that the *gabinetes fonográficos* often used as the main criticism against their competitor.[98] On the other hand, this meant gramophones were not as prone to accidental, unwanted moments in respect to live sound, such as pitch distortions. Even though the gramophones were still lacking in many ways, they were able to capture a broader range of sounds in an acceptable way than the earlier technologies.[99] For example, since recording string instruments remained difficult, gramophone recordists were able to develop effective ways of recording singers accompanied by small brass orchestras. This is the kind of accompaniment – as opposed to piano – that we hear in most *zarzuela* recordings from the period. Gramophone discs could also capture dynamics and timbres in more realistic ways, which opens up the possibility that some of the compensation mechanisms discussed in the previous section when it came to recording *zarzuela* numbers might have evolved or even disappeared. In the context of these slightly later disc recordings, the choral recording of 'Salve' from *Gigantes y cabezudos* discussed in the previous section stands out as an anomaly, which suggests that such widespread use of portamento was not the norm and might have been used to address a specific technical-technological problem, namely overemphasizing one expressive device which recorded well (i.e., portamento) to compensate for ones that did not.

Since *zarzuela* could not be easily recorded anywhere else but in Spain (with some isolated exceptions in Latin and North America), it was on this repertory that the Spanish branch of Gramophone focused.[100] Other companies followed similar strategies, such as Odeon, which was established in 1903 as a label of the International Talking Machine Company, then the leading rival of Gramophone and in January 1904 became part of the Carl Lindström Company. Odeon and Gramophone became the leaders in the *zarzuela* recording market and remained so during the following decades. At the same time, recordings were starting to become a much more attractive proposition for singers, particularly after Caruso's recordings for Victor in 1904 proved that making recordings could be a lucrative career move for a performer with an already established stage reputation.

The mass-production and mass-distribution processes of multinationals meant that recordings by international celebrities could now be sold every-where. This reduced the need for local companies to produce their own

---

the bass Andrés Perelló de Segurola. Other Spanish singers made recordings but did so abroad, such as Marino Aineto, who recorded in Paris.

[98] 'Hijos de Blas Cuesta' (advertisement), *Boletín fonográfico* 27 (1901), 42.

[99] Leech-Wilkinson, *The Changing Sound of Music*, ch. 3, para. 8–10.

[100] This was also the case for other indigenous genres such as flamenco and choral arrangements of traditional songs.

recordings. For some time after 1904, Gramophone kept hiring some of the singers it had employed in its earlier years, such as Rafael Bezares (a singer with a very prolific recording career), but the company gradually changed its hiring practices to fall in line with the rest of the industry. As a result, recording *zarzuela* became increasingly concentrated in the hands of a much smaller number of performers than before. These were now normally singers who had achieved success on stage, many of whom were part of a new generation of performers who began their careers after the era of the *gabinetes*. They included the husband and wife team of baritone Emilio Sagi Barba and *tiple* Luisa Vela,[101] baritone Inocencio Navarro and tenor José Palet. These singers form the first generation of *zarzuela* singers who from the start consistently made recordings integral to their professional careers. In this new era of recording technology, we can assume that particular choices in terms of performance practice do not necessarily mean a lack of ability on the part of the singer, but rather are conscious decisions.

Apart from changes in recording technology and the recording industry itself, it is likely that the dynamics within the *zarzuela* sphere also contributed to these developments. Around 1900, *género chico* started to decline in popularity, which led to the rise of the so-called *géneros frívolos*. These were comparable to non-narrative genres from outside Spain such as music hall, cabaret and vaudeville. The most important subgenres of *géneros frívolos* were *cuplé* and *variedade*. A *cuplé* consisted of a single song, normally sung by a female performer, that was often erotic in nature and therefore capitalized on the singer's sexualized stage presence. *Variedades* offered a series of singing, dancing and comedy numbers, usually performed by different artists, that were sometimes tied very loosely to a common topic.[102]

---

[101] Vela, while a teenager, recorded a few cylinders for *gabinetes* in Valencia as an amateur performer before embarking on her stage career in the early years of the twentieth century ('Jugar con fuego', *La correspondencia de España*, 29 November 1902; 'Debut de señorita Vela', *El defensor de Córdoba*, 24 October 1903). She was also a noted performer of the title role in Franz Lehár's *Die lustige Witwe* (The Merry Widow), which further confirms how *zarzuela* existed in an ecosystem of multiple genres.

[102] Earlier histories of *género chico* (e.g., Matilde Muñoz, *Historia de la zarzuela y el género chico* (Madrid: Tesoro, 1946); José Deleito y Piñuela, *Origen y apogeo del 'género chico'* (Madrid: Revista de Occidente, 1949); Marciano Zurita, *Historia del género chico* (Madrid: Prensa Popular, 1920)) typically end either before the appearance of *géneros frívolos* or by mentioning them dismissively. Dramatically and structurally, *géneros frívolos* differed from *género chico* and *zarzuela* more generally, since, even though they still relied on their stage component, they consisted of separate unconnected numbers. However, continuities between *género chico* and the *géneros frívolos* have been highlighted in more recent scholarship. See, for example, Serge Salaün, 'Cuplé y variedades (1890–1915)', in Serge Salaün, Evelyne Ricci and Marie Salgues, eds., *La escena española en la encrucijada (1890–1910)* (Madrid: Espiral Hispanoamericana, 2005), 125–151.

Alongside the flourishing of the *géneros frívolos*, longer-format *zarzuela* was experiencing a significant revival. Thanks to influences from French, Austro-Germanic and English operetta styles, the genre experienced a resurgence with works such as Amadeo Vives's *Maruxa* (1914), José Serrano's *La canción del olvido* (1916) and Pablo Luna's *El asombro de Damasco* (1916) and *El niño judío* (1918). Operettas such as *Die lustige Witwe* (The Merry Widow) and *Die Dollarprinzessin* (The Dollar Princess) were also sometimes performed by *zarzuela* companies in Spanish translation (as *La viuda alegre* and *La princesa del dóla,* respectively). Performers such as the aforementioned Sagi Barba, Vela and Navarro, among others, rose to fame as the champions of the renewed *zarzuela grande* and some, such as Vela, also appeared regularly in translated operettas.

After 1910, the *zarzuela* scene was, in some respects, the opposite of what it had been for the past three decades. New *zarzuelas grandes* were regularly appearing, with different levels of success. They were often produced by companies managed by the *zarzuela* composers themselves. A handful of these new *zarzuelas* remained in the repertoire, but audiences were not as drawn to new *zarzuelas grandes* as they once had been. This meant that impresarios had to program audience favourites alongside new works as a hopeful guarantee for a season's overall commercial success. Familiar titles, it was hoped, would cover the costs for new works, which may not recoup their own expenses. Audiences continued to be drawn to past favourites such as *Marina* (Emilio Arrieta), *La tempestad* (Ruperto Chapí), *El juramento* (Joaquín Gaztambide), *El salto del pasiego* (Manuel Fernández Caballero) and *Jugar con fuego* (Francisco Asenjo Barbieri).[103] *Zarzuela* was starting to become increasingly dependent on its past repertoire, rather than on new works. This was especially evident in *género chico*, which by 1910 had practically become fossilized. Earlier successes such as *La revoltosa*, *Gigantes y cabezudos* and *La gran vía* remained popular and an almost certain guarantee of success for any *zarzuela* company. The subgenre was now being seen more as a window to the past of the Spanish *pueblo* rather than a living art form.[104]

The changing balance between *género chico* and *zarzuela grande* had a definite impact on the working patterns of singers and companies. Even though some theatres such as the Apolo in Madrid performed only *género chico*, during this period it became increasingly less common for companies to specialize in a single subgenre. Singers had to adapt to the new circumstances and perform from both repertoires while also making recordings. To some

---

[103] Anonymous, 'La vida musical', *El arte musical*, 30 September 1917, 66.
[104] Sorozábal, *Mi vida y mi obra*, 224–225.

extent, their recordings reached international audiences through Victor's Blue and Black labels and, later, on His Master's Voice (as the Gramophone Co. became known). *Zarzuela*, unlike flamenco, never became globally popular; hence, the number of *zarzuela* recordings made outside Spain remained very small and usually featured well-known numbers performed by singers from other Spanish-speaking countries, such as the US baritone (of Spanish ancestry) Emilio de Gogorza, the Mexican baritone José Torres Ovando and the Mexican soprano Soledad Goyzueta. These singers typically did not have the experience of performing *zarzuela* on stage, unlike their contemporaries in Spain. They typically recorded other genres besides *zarzuela*, most often opera and Spanish-language song. Among the recordings made in Spain, only a small percentage made it into the multinationals' global catalogues. Those that did sold mostly in Latin America and among Spanish-speaking communities in the United States. While it cannot in any way be said that Spanish singers changed their performance styles for the international market, it is likely that the increased distribution of recordings had an impact on their availability and quality and vice versa. With recordists increasingly acquiring experience through trial and error and star singers replacing lesser-known ones, recordings produced after 1905 would have had a better chance than their predecessors to succeed in international markets. At the same time, opportunities to enter such global marketplaces might have provided an incentive for recordists and performers to make sure that what they produced was of a very high standard.

When it comes to portamento, gramophone recordings from the early 1900s to the years around the First World War largely confirm and deepen our understanding of the practices preserved on wax cylinders. The greater number of surviving recordings offer further evidence of the different expressive possibilities associated with portamento at this time. This is evident in the soprano romanza 'Pensar en él', from *Marina*, which María Darnís recorded for Gramophone in 1914.[105] The opening section ('Pensar en él/esa es mi vida') uses portamento sparsely and, interestingly, mostly on smaller intervals of a second or a third. This aligns with the rather declamatory quality of Darnís's voice in this passage. Portamento, following the observations of Leech-Wilkinson and Potter cited above, contributes to the overall impression of spoken speech. Portamentos become more numerous in the final section, in which they appear on practically every descending interval of a third or larger. This allows Darnís's performance to take on a more sung and less spoken quality.

---

[105] María Darnís, 'Pensar en él', by Emilio Arrieta, recorded for Gramophone in 1914, matrix no. 063041, digitization not available.

The greater numbers of surviving discs as well as the audible improvements in technology provide us with greater understanding of the hybridity of *zarzuela* and how this hybridity was expressed through performance practice. In the previous section, I discussed how portamento tended to be absent from the recordings of singers whose mode of vocal production was closer to that associated with popular genres, with clear diction and little vibrato. Recordings from the gramophone era confirm that operatic and more popular styles were not two separate categories but rather formed a continuum. Singers were typically placed along this spectrum based upon their technical skill, their vocal habits and preferences and their ability to access a bespoke range of expressive resources.

Two *zarzuelas* that were being recorded with increasing frequency during these years, both of which support this assertion, are Tomás Bretón's *La verbena de la Paloma* (1894) and Federico Chueca's *La gran vía* (1886). Both are classic examples of *género chico*. Set in Madrid, they feature a range of relatable, if generally unheroic, characters from the urban *pueblo*. As such, they might have invited less operatic, more spoken approaches to performance. Written evidence suggests that this was the case at their premieres, with 'singing actors' rather than trained singers cast in some of the main roles.[106] But discs show that a range of approaches to these works coexisted at the time. In Pilar Perales's 1917 recording of *La verbena*'s *señá* Rita – a stereotypical working class matron – for Gramophone, the singer's vibrato is appreciable and so is the uniformity of her registers. Portamento is not overly prominent, but when it does appear, it is quick and well-executed. Furthermore, following convention in more substantial romanzas, it appears at the ends of phrases.[107] Manuel Fernández Carbonell's 1922 recording of *La Gran Vía's* 'Vals del caballero de Gracia', by contrast, shows a different approach to combining distinctive performance elements, including portamento, in order to create an expressive performance.[108] Fernández Carbonell's vocal placement clearly features a low soft palate. His solid diction would have surely met the requirements of *naturalismo*. The singer's portamentos, however, go against the expectations of Manuel García and other famed singing teachers, who thought that portamento should be executed with proper breath support and a uniformity of tone. Some of Fernández Carbonell's portamentos sound like they are dragging,[109]

---

[106] Moreda Rodríguez, 'Singing and Speaking in Early Twentieth-Century *Zarzuela*', 39.

[107] Pilar Perales, señor Gandía, Vicente Carrión and Gonzalito, 'Canción de Julián', by Tomás Bretón, recorded for Gramophone in 1917, catalogue no. 0264005, http://bdh.bne.es/bnesearch/detalle/bdh0000105463.

[108] Manuel Fernández Carbonell, 'Vals del caballero de Gracia', by Federico Chueca, recorded for International Talking Machine in 1922, matrix no. SO 756, http://bdh.bne.es/bnesearch/detalle/bdh0000167379 (Cara A).

[109] At 0:38 and 1:10, above.

Figure 4 'Vals del Caballero de Gracia' from Federico Chueca's *La Gran Vía*, bars 32–40, as written (4a) and as performed (4b) by Manuel Fernández Carbonell

while others appear almost like sighs.[110] Still others hint at a very subtle drop in pitch at the end of the note.[111] It is the latter two characteristics in particular that connect Fernández Carbonell's performance to the comments by Leech-Wilkinson and Potter about portamento and spoken language. These portamentos sit halfway between spontaneous asides that might come up in everyday speech and intentional musical artifice.

Fernández Carbonell's performance certainly stands out for its spoken quality. Apart from the vocal production and diction, the singer shows an outstanding ability to intelligently shorten or elongate syllables in order to craft an expressive performance (see Figure 4). If we recall the 1902 anonymous recording of 'Canción de Paloma' discussed above, we can observe some of the same performance techniques. Fernández Carbonell's overall rendition, however, strikes us as more musical, with its alleged shortcomings actually being used to its advantage. This might be simply because Fernández Carbonell had a greater sense of musicianship than the 1902 singer or it could be because, by this time, performers such as himself would be more experienced in studio practices and increasingly aware of how different performance elements could complement each other.

---

[110] At 1:35, above.　　[111] At 1:42, above.

A further revelation coming from these pre-electrical discs that furthers our understanding of *zarzuela*'s hybridity is the appearance of what we might call comic portamento. Comic portamentos were normally performed by a comic or lower class character or in a comic situation. They normally occur on larger intervals (fourths, fifths) rather than on smaller ones and when compared to a standard portamento, they tend to appear more often on ascending intervals than on descending ones. Moreover, there tends to be something in the way comic portamento is performed that invites laughter: comic portamento deviates from expectations about well-executed portamentos in such an exaggerated way that it cannot be anything other than deliberate. Sometimes, for example, the second note is stressed (whereas in regular portamento, it would normally be the first), which makes the portamento sound like a sort of springboard from the lower to the higher note rather than as a subtle slide from one note to the next.[112] Sometimes the portamento is executed with an obvious, hyperbolic crescendo. On other occasions, comic portamentos sound like exaggerated versions of legato that in turn try to mimic certain intonations associated with lower class characters, such as slurred speech. This is the case in a recording of *La Gran Vía*'s 'Jota de los ratas' recorded by Ernesto Hervás, Rafael Alaria and Rafael Díaz for Gramophone in 1922.[113]

Recordings from this time also allow us to identify changes in how certain numbers were performed and how these changes might have been tied to broader debates about the cultural significance of certain *zarzuelas* and their places within the genre's canon. 'Ay de mí', the soprano *arieta* from Ruperto Chapí's *El rey que rabió*, was one of the most recorded romanzas during the gramophone era.[114] The two earliest documented recordings, those by Antonietta Martínez (1899)[115] and

---

[112] Such as Luisa Vela and Emilio Sagi Barba, 'Soy un pastor sencillo', by Ruperto Chapí, recorded for Gramophone in 1915, matrix no. 64410, http://bdh.bne.es/bnesearch/detalle/bdh0000012856 (Cara B), at 0:14, 0:19, 0:25 and 0:35. Here, the effect is compounded by several portamentos appearing in a short space of time.

[113] Ernesto Hervás, Rafael Alaria and Rafael Díaz, 'Terceto de los ratas', by Federico Chueca, recorded for International Talking Machine in 1922, matrix no. SO 851, http://bdh.bne.es/bnesearch/detalle/bdh0000167379 (Cara B); see 2:25, 2:33.

[114] Additional recordings beyond those discussed here include ones by Marina Gurina, 'El rey que rabió: Arieta', by Ruperto Chapí, recorded for Gramophone and Typewriter in 1902, matrix no. 63284; Blanca del Carmen, 'El rey que rabió: Aire', by Ruperto Chapí, recorded for Zonophone ca. 1902, matrix no. 7070; Angelita Homs, 'El rey que rabió (Chapí)', by Ruperto Chapí, recorded for Gramophone in 1905, matrix no. 63625; Teresita Silva, 'El rey que rabió: Romanza', by Ruperto Chapí, recorded for Gramophone in 1906, matrix no. 63680; Carmen Domingo, 'El rey que rabió: Romanza', by Ruperto Chapí, recorded for Gramophone in 1909, no matrix no.

[115] Antonietta Martínez, 'El rey que rabió (Chapí)', by Ruperto Chapí, recorded for Gramophone in 1899, matrix no. 3395, https://yalemusiclib.aviaryplatform.com/collections/213/collection_re sources/12900.

Emilia Colás (1902),[116] both feature a strong spoken quality. Despite technological issues, particularly with the Colás recording, the performers demonstrate relatively intelligible diction, which suggests a low soft palate technique. Tempos in both recordings are brisk and steady and portamento is scarce. All in all, the perform-ances are highly reminiscent of those of popular and traditional songs, such as Roque's 'Seguidillas' from *Marina* described above. A contemporary recording by Soledad Goyzueta, made in the United States for Edison Gold Moulded Records in 1904, also features strong spoken elements (diction remains relatively clear throughout), though – by contrast – she employs a more consistent use of vibrato as well as operatic vocal technique.[117]

In the following decade, recordings by Emilia Vergerí (1910)[118] and Luisa Vela 1915)[119] of the same romanza reflect a large-scale shift in approach. Both singers, following Goyzueta, employ modes of vocal production that are more operatic in style, with a high soft palate and more constant vibrato. They are not identical, for Vergerí's voice is lighter and Vela's is more lyrical. The tempo on these recordings is considerably slower than on the two earlier ones (and also slightly slower than Goyzueta's), which allows for greater fluctuations in tempo fluctuation and a more generous use of portamento, particularly at the ends of stanzas (see Figure 5).

The differences between the earlier and later recordings suggest that a reconceptualization of the role of Rosa in *El rey que rabió* might have been happening on Spanish stages at this time, one that reflected not only the hybridity of the genre but also shifts in its fundamental aesthetics. *El rey que rabió* is a full length *zarzuela*, with significant comic and even grotesque elements, alongside an import-ant presence of the *pueblo*. The plot follows a young king (a trouser role) who is intent on finding out how his subjects really live by mixing with them, *incognito*, in a range of situations. The approach followed by Colás and Martínez in the earlier recordings would have served to emphasize Rosa's humble origins, making her more akin to *género chico* female characters in her simplicity and lack of artifice. Vela's and Vergerí's interpretations, on the other hand, would have emphasized her status as a dramatic heroine, someone who has to overcome a number of obstacles to finally marry the king. This gives a sense of gravitas to the character at a time when full-length *zarzuelas*, both new and old, were returning to fashion.

---

[116] Emilia Colás, 'El rey que rabió: Romanza (Chapí)', by Ruperto Chapí, recorded for Zonophone in 1902, matrix no. 1114, http://bdh.bne.es/bnesearch/detalle/bdh0000167367).

[117] Soledad Goyzueta, 'El rey que rabió: Romanza', by Ruperto Chapí, recorded for Edison Gold Moulded Records in 1904, no. 18541, https://cylinders.library.ucsb.edu/detail.php?query_type=mms_id&query=990046978900203776&r=21&of=25.

[118] Emilia Vergerí, 'Ay de mí: Romanza', by Ruperto Chapí, recorded for Gramophone in 1910, matrix no. 4230, http://bdh.bne.es/bnesearch/detalle/bdh0000180878, Cara A.

[119] Luisa Vela, 'Romanza Ay de mí', by Ruperto Chapí, recorded for Gramophone in 1915, matrix no. S-18996, http://bdh.bne.es/bnesearch/detalle/bdh0000177780, Cara A.

Figure 5 'Ay de mí' from Ruperto Chapí's *El rey que rabió*, bars 27–33, with portamentos added to reflect the performances of Emilia Vergerí (5a) and Luisa Vela (5b)

Electrical Recording Takes Over, 1925–1936

The introduction of electrical recording in the mid 1920s ignited a seismic paradigm shift in the recording industry. The ways in which the sounds of voices and instruments were captured improved significantly and listening to recordings became a more aesthetically satisfying experience.[120] What one could listen to in the comfort of one's own home was not just closer to reality in terms of fidelity than it had been previously, but it was experienced in a way that was more real than reality, for listeners could now appreciate nuances that might have gone unnoticed in the concert hall or theatre.[121] These technical improvements, therefore, began to redefine listening practices worldwide. Prolonged, solitary listening for pleasure became a much more compelling experience than it had been just a few years earlier. Hence, the persona of the discophile (or record listener) – a keen listener equally interested in the technological and artistic aspects of recorded sound – started to emerge.[122]

---

[120] Leech-Wilkinson, *The Changing Sound of Music*, ch. 3, para. 28.

[121] Sophie Maisonneuve, 'La Voix de son Maître: Entre corps et technique, l'avènement d'une écoute musicale nouvelle au XXe siècle', *Communications* 81 (2007): 47–59, especially 54–57.

[122] Sophie Maisonneuve, 'La constitution d'une culture et d'une écoute musicale nouvelles: Le disque et ses sociabilités comme agents de changement culturel dans les années 1920 et 1930 en Grande-Bretagne', *Revue de Musicologie* 88 (2002): 43–66, especially 44–45.

In many respects, the technical differences between pre-electrical and electrical recordings favour the latter, even when filtered through the prism of digitization. We can hypothesize that these technological advances must have been even more striking to 1920s listeners, recordists and singers, especially since they resulted in quick, immediately noticeable changes in how *zarzuela* recordings were being made. Voices could now be captured more accurately, which made for more realistic and pleasurable listening experiences without the shrillness that was sometimes present in the past when recording higher voices. The new technology was also much better for recording string instruments and so there was a shift from the brass arrangements used to accompany singers on cylinder recordings back to the original string-dominated orchestrations. Dynamics were also given a new lease of life, as it was now possible to record with greater accuracy the *filados* (e.g., a crescendo followed by a decrescendo, as in the Italian *messa di voce*) that some of the most technically competent singers added to their use of portamento. Prime examples of this technique can be heard in recordings by the baritone Marcos Redondo, one of the most celebrated *zarzuela* performers of the time and also a prolific recording artist.[123] Recordings by Redondo and his contemporaries suggest that the relationship between recorded and live music was again being renegotiated. Technological advancements would have allowed singers to take their stage mannerisms into the recording studio without needing to compensate as much for the loss of certain aspects of live performance, such as dynamics. For example, in recordings from the early electrical era, tempo modifications occur less frequently than in previous recordings and when they do appear, the rate of acceleration or deceleration tends to be less.

In other respects, the impact of electrical recordings on performance styles and the listening experience was more gradual and broadly based. Recordings were intertwined with a range of musical, cultural and social developments that transpired over years or even decades. The early years of electrical recording took place during a particularly fruitful time for *zarzuela grande*. Amadeu

---

[123] Redondo sang, recorded and gained popular and critical acclaim for his renditions of all the major baritone roles in both the newer and the classic *zarzuela* repertoires (e.g., *Marina*, *La tempestad*, *Luisa Fernanda*, *La del soto del parral*). Among his most important recordings are 'Romanza de Juan Eguía' from *La tabernera del puerto* by Pablo Sorozábal, recorded in 1936 for Odeón, matrix no. SO 8790, digitization not available; with Ángeles Ottein, 'En mi tierra extremeña' from *Luisa Fernanda* by Federico Moreno Torroba, recorded in 1933 for Odeón, matrix no. SO 7637, http://bdh.bne.es/bnesearch/detalle/bdh0000171237 (Cara B); with Conchita Supervía, 'La revoltosa: Dúo' from *La revoltosa* by Ruperto Chapí, recorded in 1931 for Odeón, matrix nos. SO 6053, SO 6054, http://bdh.bne.es/bnesearch/detalle/bdh0000015223 (Cara A and B); and 'Monólogo' from *La tempestad* by Ruperto Chapí, recorded in 1931 for Odeón, matrix nos. XXS 4649, XXS 4950, http://bdh.bne.es/bnesearch/detalle/bdh0000008279 (Cara A and B).

Vives, after some successes in the second decade of the century, went on to write what is perhaps his best-known work today, *Doña Francisquita*, in 1923. Other noted composers were also establishing themselves in the newly thriving genre, including the team of Reveriano Soutullo and Juan Vert (*La del soto del parral* (1927)) and Jacinto Guerrero (*Los gavilanes* (1924) and *El huésped del sevillano* (1926)). The first half of the 1930s (more specifically, until the beginning of the Spanish Civil War in 1936) saw the rise of two composers who came to dominate Spanish theatrical life at the time and who can be rightly described as the two last great *zarzuelistas*: Pablo Sorozábal (1897–1988), who brought influences from German expressionist theatre into the genre and Federico Moreno Torroba (1891–1982), who followed a more traditional style.[124] New *zarzuelas* were constantly appearing (though not at the same rate as in the glory years of *género chico*) and several became instant classics. For example, *Doña Francisquita* had sixty performances in Valencia alone during the five months following its premiere.[125] Within another four months, it had been performed three hundred times throughout Spain.[126] Other *zarzuelas* enjoyed similar success, including the previously discussed *La del soto del parral*, *Los gavilanes* and *El huésped del sevillano*, as well as Sorozábal's *Katiuska* (1931), *La del manojo del rosas* (1934) and *La tabernera del puerto* (1936) and Moreno Torroba's *Luisa Fernanda* (1932). And there were some surprises. Even though early predictions for the success of *La del manojo de rosas* were not optimistic, Sorozábal claimed in his 1986 memoir that after its premiere not a month went by without at least one performance of the work, which led to more than 15,000 performances over the following decades.[127]

These new *zarzuelas* appeared alongside earlier works such as *Gigantes y cabezudos*, *La revoltosa*, *La verbena de la Paloma*, *Marina* and *La tempestad*. Notably, some of the older, more classic zarzuelas such as Asenjo Barbieri's *El barberillo de Lavapiés* and *Jugar con fuego* were rarely performed,[128] although they were still seen as staples of the genre. (These works would not be revived until the 1950s.) Furthermore, several *zarzuelas* that were popular during the 1920s and 1930s (e.g., *El bateo, La reina mora* and *El anillo de hierro*) remain obscure nowadays. It is likely that recordings played a part in this, for these works were recorded less often than others. Recordings, therefore, did not simply mirror what the repertoire was at any given point in time but also contributed to shaping it.

---

[124] Mario Lerena, 'De Berlín a Madrid, o la huella del teatro musical germánico en la obra temprana de Pablo Sorozábal Mariezkurrena', *Cuadernos de música iberoamericana*, 18 (2009): 38.

[125] Anonymous, 'Teatro Ruzafa', *El pueblo*, 29 March 1924, 3.

[126] Anonymous, 'Doña Francisquita', *El Eco de Santiago,* 4 August 1924, 2.

[127] Sorozábal, *Mi vida y mi obra*, 231.

[128] Anonymous, 'Los teatros: NTRO', *El liberal*, 23 August 1929.

One consequence of the gradual standardization of *a zarzuela* repertoire was that singers did not have to learn new works at the same pace as did their earlier counterparts in *género chico*. Furthermore, they could afford to specialize in a handful of roles. For example, Vendrell claimed that he made his career on the basis of five works,[129] while Redondo kept an active repertoire of twenty-five works.[130] These were only fractions of what performers would have been expected to know a generation earlier. Thus, many of the singers we hear in recordings from the early electrical era were singing roles they had performed hundreds of times on stage, whereas this level of familiarity with the part is not always the case for some of the singers heard on pre-electrical recordings.

It was also in the mid 1920s that recording companies systematically started to record and release albums that included the principal musical numbers from a particular *zarzuela*. These sets consisted of six, eight or ten sides sold together. Whereas it is difficult to pinpoint a direct cause-and-effect relationship between the appearance of such albums and the advent of electrical recordings, it is likely that the increased fidelity and possibilities for aesthetic enjoyment achievable through electrical recordings made such releases more appealing to consumers who were becoming more accustomed to solitary listening. Many *zarzuelas* that had successful stage premieres were recorded almost immediately thereafter in this album format, some of them several times within a few years. This was the case, for example, with both *Doña Francisquita*[131] and *Luisa Fernanda*.[132] These were not complete recordings by any means. Dialogue was omitted, as

---

[129] Vendrell, *El cant*, 25.

[130] Redondo, *Un hombre que se va*, 155.

[131] The following list of recordings of *Doña Francisquita* includes, in this order, the names of the singers singing Francisquita, Fernando, Aurora la Beltrana and Cardona and the conductor (when known): Amparo Alarcón, Emili Vendrell, Cora Raga and Ricardo Fuentes, *Doña Francisquita*, by Amadeo Vives, recorded for Odeón in 1924; Mary Isaura, Juan de Casenave, Cora Raga and Antonio Palacios, *Doña Francisquita*, by Amadeo Vives, recorded for Odeón in 1924; Mary Isaura, Juan Rosich, Cora Raga, Antonio Palacios and Concordio Gelabert, *Doña Francisquita*, by Amadeo Vives, recorded for Odeón in 1925; Felisa Herrero, Emili Vendrell, Sélica Pérez Carpio, Antonio Palacios and Antonio Olaizola, *Doña Francisquita*, by Amadeo Vives, recorded by Columbia-Regal in 1930.

[132] The following list of recordings of *Luisa Fernanda* includes, in this order, the names of the singers singing Luisa Fernanda, Duquesa Carolina, Javier and Vidal and the conductor: Ángeles Ottein, Emili Vendrell, Marcos Redondo, E. Acevedo y Puri, *Luisa Fernanda*, by Federico Moreno Torroba, recorded for Odeón in 1932; Laura Nieto, Tino Folgar, Emilio Sagi Barba and Federico Moreno Torroba, *Luisa Fernanda*, by Federico Moreno Torroba, recorded for Odeón in 1933; Sélica Perez Carpio, Faustino Arregui, Marcos Redondo and E. Acevedo y Puri, *Luisa Fernanda*, by Federico Moreno Torroba, recorded for Regal in 1934. The characters Luisa Fernanda and Duquesa Carolina do not sing any numbers together (although they appear together in dialogue scenes) and so it was possible for the same singer to sing both parts on the same recording, which would not have been the usual practice in a stage production.

were some of the less important numbers and those that would be the most difficult to record, such as ensembles requiring multiple singers.

Although the production of albums that included selections from a single *zarzuela* was presumably driven by commercial rather than artistic reasons, it eventually had an impact on performance practice. Record companies did not just piece together sides that a few years earlier would have simply been sold separately. Evidence from the recordings themselves suggests that the idea of the album as an artistic artifact (and not just a commercial product) was starting to develop at this time. Some singers were beginning to think beyond individual numbers in the studio and were developing performing and interpretive strategies that would shape the evolution of their characters throughout the album, just as they would likely have done on stage.

One particularly illustrative example of this interpretative approach can be heard in the multiple recordings of *Luisa Fernanda* that were made in the early 1930s. Act 2 of this immensely popular *zarzuela* opens with the well-known 'Mazurka de las sombrillas', in which the people of Madrid flock to the hermitage of San Antonio de la Florida to celebrate the annual *romería*. *Damiselas* (young women) and *pollos* (young men) flirt with each other nonchalantly. In the midst of the choral revelry, Javier and the duchess Carolina enter and sing a short duet. Throughout the whole scene and subsequent developments, Carolina – a staunch monarchist – attempts to present herself as a non-aristocrat who understands and even participates in several of the events in the life of the *pueblo*. Some recorded performances of the duet attempt to show this aspect of her persona through performance practice. Ángeles Ottein, in her 1932 Odeón recording, avoids portamento in ways that sound very deliberate,[133] especially when compared with her performances of other numbers in the *zarzuela*, for which she does use portamento.[134] Furthermore, her contemporaries Laura Nieto,[135] Sélica Pérez Carpio[136] and Regina Zaldívar[137] all employ

---

[133] Emili Vendrell and Ángeles Ottein, 'Mazurca de las sombrillas', by Federico Moreno Torroba, recorded in 1932 for Odeón, matrix no. SO 7621, http://bdh.bne.es/bnesearch/detalle/bdh0000179125 (Cara B, 1:32; please note that the BDH entry incorrectly gives the names of Esperanza Arquero and Eloy Parra, who sing other roles in the same recording).

[134] Ángeles Ottein, Emili Vendrell and Marcos Redondo, 'Caballero del alto plumero' and 'Terceto', by Federico Moreno Torroba, recorded in 1932 for Odeón, matrix nos. SO 7672, SO 7671, http://bdh.bne.es/bnesearch/detalle/bdh0000179121 (Caras A and B).

[135] Tino Folgar and Laura Nieto, 'Mazurca de las sombrillas', by Federico Moreno Torroba, recorded in 1933 for Odeón, matrix no. OJ 380, http://bdh.bne.es/bnesearch/detalle/bdh0000173109 (Cara B, 1:20).

[136] Faustino Arregui and Sélica Pérez Carpio, 'Mazurca de las sombrillas', by Federico Moreno Torroba, recorded in 1933 or Gramophone, KI 2917, http://bdh.bne.es/bnesearch/detalle/bdh0000175429 (Cara B, 1:44).

[137] Pepe Romeu and Regina Zaldívar, 'Mazurca de las sombrillas', by Pablo Sorozábal, recorded for Columbia Graphophone in 1932, matrix K 3071, http://bdh.bne.es/bnesearch/detalle/bdh0000170735 (Cara B, 1:08).

Figure 6 'Mazurka de las sombrillas', bars 83–91, from Federico Moreno Torroba's *Luisa Fernanda*, as written (and performed by Ángeles Ottein) (6a) and as performed by Laura Nieto, Sélica Pérez Carpio and Regina Zaldívar (6b)

portamento in the 'Mazurca' (see Figure 6). Ottein, therefore, stands out for her deliberate avoidance of portamento as a means to show her solidarity with the *pueblo*. These other performers, however, employ other expressive techniques to show their connection with the ways of the *pueblo*. Nieto's interpretation, for example, features a very distinctive spoken quality, with clear diction and a brisk, excited tempo that avoids the tempo modifications typical of the time. In all four recordings, Javier and the chorus (made up of young men and women from the upper classes who, like Carolina, have come to the festival to experience an aspect of *pueblo* life) make extensive use of portamento. This prominence makes Ottein as Carolina's avoidance of the technique all the more obvious and perhaps even comic, as the other outsider characters do not seem as over-keen as she is to fit in.

Beyond these interpretive uses of portamento, which require comparison between different numbers from the same *zarzuela* or multiple performances of the same number to become apparent, individual recordings also show some substantial shifts in performance practice when compared to earlier cylinders and discs. Indeed, the 1920s saw what emerges as the greatest documented change thus far in how portamento was used in *zarzuela*. By now, portamento had become a fundamental vocal technique for singers. It appeared more often but also more discreetly and played a significant role in defining the decidedly more legato approach that characterizes recordings of this era. At the same time, in some contexts it remained a device that could be used intentionally for specific expressive purposes. These roles of portamento become increasingly differentiated, not just in terms of how the portamento was executed but also in terms of how often it appeared. The former type, which I call portamento-legato, became more common, whereas the latter one, which I call expressive portamento, became rarer, subtler and more streamlined.

Unlike the uses of portamento discussed earlier, portamento-legato was applied to smaller intervals (e.g., seconds and thirds) and often appeared in all or most of the smaller intervals in a phrase. In recordings, it is often performed in a non-emphatic manner, which makes it seem more like a default or background consideration rather than a precise expressive gesture used to highlight a particular dramatic moment.[138] Singing manuals from the electrical era suggest that this awareness of portamento as an aid to legato had increased in the intervening decade. The famed *zarzuela* tenor Emili Vendrell and the Spanish operatic tenor Hipólito Lázaro (who occasionally performed in *zarzuela*) expressed similar views in their books on singing technique. Lázaro recommends singing a legato four-note scale, using portamento to connect the notes, in order to help develop the *passaggio*[139] and Vendrell describes a similar exercise.[140]

During the early electrical era, portamento-legato can sometimes be heard on larger ascending and descending intervals. One outstanding example is the descending fifth on the word 'imagen' (image) in Emili Vendrell's recording of Fernando's romanza 'Por el humo se sabe dónde está el fuego' from *Doña Francisquita* (see Figure 7). The portamento is understated, almost like a natural consequence of Vendrell emphasizing the highest pitch (on 'ma') of the three-syllable word, which he executes in an elegant, controlled manner.[141]

Expressive portamento, on the other hand, showed more continuity with previous practices. It was typically applied to larger intervals, descending rather than ascending, and appeared at the ends of phrases rather than at the

---

[138] There are certainly instances of portamento being used in this way in some recordings from between 1896 and 1924. In a wax cylinder choral recording from the *gabinete* Corrons, the continuous portamento-legato might have been achieved through experimentation (e.g., López-Marán in Señor Pretel and Eloísa López Marán, '¡Por Dios!, ¡tu pena cese!' from *Marina*, by Emilio Arrieta, recorded by Sociedad Fonográfica Española Hugens y Acosta around 1900, no matrix or publication number, http://bdh.bne.es/bnesearch/detalle/bdh0000046264; and Florencio Constantino, 'Costas las del Levante' from *Marina*, by Emilio Arrieta, recorded by Odeón in 1906, matrix no. 41206. no digitization available). Similar instances also appear in solo recordings, often from singers with operatic experience.

[139] Hipólito Lázaro, *Mi método de canto* (Madrid: Imprenta Agustín Núñez, 1947), 33.

[140] Vendrell, *El cant*, 114.

[141] Emili Vendrell, 'Romanza de Fernando' from *Doña Francisquita*, by Amadeo Vives, recorded in 1924 for Odeón, matrix no. XXS 2116, http://bdh.bne.es/bnesearch/detalle/bdh0000175406 (Cara B, 1:40).

del al - ma va sa - lien - do lai - ma - gen muer - ta

Figure 7 'Por el humo se sabe dónde está el fuego' from *Doña Francisquita*, bars 43–44, as performed by Emili Vendrell

yaun sin a - mor

Figure 8 'Pensar en él', from *Marina*, bars 87–88, as performed by Mercedes Capsir for Columbia Graphophone in 1930

beginnings. It was used less frequently than in earlier eras and was often executed in ways that resonate better with our modern sensibilities, namely with more consistent breath support and with a quicker and more agile motion. Furthermore, a new general practice emerged: an ascending portamento would be followed by a descending one, particularly in cadential gestures where the middle note receives additional weight through a fermata, whether notated or not. This idea is clearly heard in Mercedes Capsir's recording of 'Pensar en él' from *Marina* made in 1930[142] (see Figure 8).

There are also instances in which, instead of sliding, the singer clearly articulates every diatonic pitch between the top and the bottom notes. This practice appears in contexts that otherwise would have been ripe for portamento, such as on a descending fourth at the end of a phrase (see Figure 9). It makes sense, therefore, to consider these instances as variations on the expressive portamento, one which perhaps could be regarded as a safer option for singers who did not feel secure in convincingly executing a slide.[143]

As in the past, portamento did not operate in isolation. Changes in its usage can only be understood within the context of broader shifts in the genre's overall performance practice. It was at the same time that electrical recording was being introduced that the mode of vocal production common in *zarzuela* recordings nowadays was also emerging. This is characterized by a high soft palate and a low larynx and, consequently, more constant vibrato and less naturalistic diction. In other words, it is at this time that *zarzuela* recordings begin to sound more and more like opera recordings. This matches our perceptions in

[142] Mercedes Capsir, 'Pensar en él' from *Marina*, by Emilio Arrieta, recorded by Columbia in 1930, matrix no. KX 173, http://bdh.bne.es/bnesearch/detalle/bdh0000178015 (Cara A).

[143] Salud Rodríguez, 'Cuarteto' from *Agua, azucarillos y aguardiente*, by Federico Chueca, recorded by Gramophone in 1929, matrix no. 2339, no digitization available.

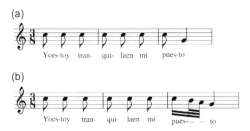

Figure 9 Quartet from *Agua, azucarillos y aguardiente*, bars 38–40, as written (9a) and as performed (9b) by Salud Rodríguez for Gramophone in 1929

2024 of how *zarzuela* should sound. Some forms of 'low soft palate' technique with a more nasal quality, however, survive among *cómico* (*tenor cómico, tiple cómica*) singers.[144] Vibrato was becoming part of the default vocal production, but some recordings reveal, like snapshots, that this was a time of transition. The tenor Delfín Pulido, for example, shows a remarkably consistent vibrato in his 1930 gramophone recording of *María la Tempranica*, while his partner Felisa Herrero offers a more selective use of vibrato that hearkens back to the time of earlier recordings in which vibrato was an expressive choice applied on selected notes.[145]

When it comes to portamento, there are also examples that can be labelled as transitional, for they show how old practices coexisted alongside new ones. In his 1924 recording of Fernando's romanza 'Por el humo se sabe dónde está el fuego' from *Doña Francisquita*, Juan de Casenave makes his portamento-legatos rather subtle, almost like a spontaneous attempt at mimicking through singing some of the inflections of spoken speech at this particular emotional moment.[146] Vedrell, in his recording of the same romanza from 1927, does something similar.[147]

---

[144] Moreda Rodríguez, 'Singing and Speaking in Early Twentieth-Century *Zarzuela*', 35–37.

[145] Felisa Herrero, 'La espera', by Gerónimo Giménez and Federico Moreno Torroba, recorded for Columbia in 1930, matrix. no. K 2150, http://bdh.bne.es/bnesearch/detalle/bdh0000171264, Cara A; Delfín Pulido, 'Romanza de Miguel', by Gerónimo Giménez and Federico Moreno Torroba, recorded for Columbia in 1930, matrix. no. K 2152, http://bdh.bne.es/bnesearch/detalle/bdh0000171264, Cara B; Felisa Herrero and Delfín Pulido, 'Dúo', by Gerónimo Giménez and Federico Moreno Torroba, recorded for Columbia in 1930, matrix no. K 2151, http://bdh.bne.es/bnesearch/detalle/bdh0000171263, Cara A; Felisa Herrero, 'Romanza de la Tempranica', by Gerónimo Giménez and Federico Moreno Torroba, recorded for Columbia in 1930, matrix no. K 2153, http://bdh.bne.es/bnesearch/detalle/bdh0000171263, Cara B.

[146] Juan de Casenave, 'Romanza de Fernando', by Amadeo Vives, recorded in 1924 for Odeón, digitization not available.

[147] Emilio Vendrell, 'Romanza de Fernando', by Amadeo Vives, recorded in 1927 for Odeon, matrix no. XXS 2117, http://bdh.bne.es/bnesearch/detalle/bdh0000175406 (Cara B).

By contrast, Juan García (Parlophon, 1930)[148] and Pepe Romeu (Columbia Regal, 1930)[149] are less subtle in their deliveries. To our modern ears, García's and Romeu's performances might sound overemphatic and even excessive, while Casenave's and Vendrell's come across as more palatable. The four tenors are all from basically the same generation (Casenave was born in 1888, Vendrell in 1893, García in 1896 and Romeu in 1900), so the differences in performance cannot be attributed to their relative ages. In fact, it is the two older singers in the group (Casenave and Vendrell) who embrace the newer styles. What the recordings suggest, therefore, is that younger singers were at this time experimenting with both older and newer practices. In this particular example, we might ask ourselves whether the fact that the older singers had played the role on stage,[150] while the younger ones had not, may also be significant. Casenave and Vendrell might have been more aware than García and Romeu that the introspective nature of the romanza suggested a quasi-spoken approach, which they emphasized through a more standard portamento-legato.

Vendrell, Casenave, García and Romeu were part of a generation who started their careers around the same time that electrical recording was emerging on both sides of the Atlantic.[151] This allowed some singers, such as Vendrell and Redondo, to experiment with new recording technologies from the very beginning of their careers. This generation of singers was therefore different in some respects from earlier ones and this difference likely contributed to the shifts in *zarzuela* singing at the time. Vendrell's writings, which include memoirs and singing treatises,[152] show that the singer was keen to present himself and his contemporaries as members of a dynamic, innovative generation intent on changing the way *zarzuela* was performed, one that left behind the alleged bad taste of past generations. Many of these

---

[148] Juan García, 'Romanza de Fernando', by Amadeo Vives, recorded by Parlophon in 1930, matrix no. 2-71032, http://bdh.bne.es/bnesearch/detalle/bdh0000009555 (Cara A).

[149] Pepe Romeu, 'Romanza de Fernando', by Amadeo Vives, recorded by Regal in 1931, matrix no. KX 360, http://bdh.bne.es/bnesearch/detalle/bdh0000170740 (Cara A).

[150] Casenave created the role of Fernando; however, the *zarzuela*'s composer, Amadeo Vives, quickly became dissatisfied with his performance. Vendrell started performing the role shortly thereafter and it became one of his signature roles.

[151] Examples of single numbers include Manuel Pineda, 'Los vareadores' from *La del soto del parral*, by Federico Moreno Torroba, recorded by Victor, unknown date, matrix no. 23-5186-B, https://frontera.library.ucla.edu/recordings/los-vareadores-0; Manuel Pineda, 'La bruja', from *La bruja* by Ruperto Chapí, recorded by Victor, unknown date, matrix no. 23-1592-B, https://frontera.library.ucla.edu/recordings/la-bruja-13; Onofré Vidal, 'Canto a la espada toledana', from *El huésped del sevillano*, by Jacinto Guerrero, recorded by Victor, unknown date, matrix no. BVE55817-1, https://frontera.library.ucla.edu/recordings/canto-la-espada-toledana-0; Manuel Pineda and Clara Stock, 'Mazurca de las sombrillas', from *Luisa Fernanda*, by Federico Moreno Torroba, recorded by Victor, unknown date, matrix no. 23-5186-A, https://frontera.library.ucla.edu/recordings/mazurca-de-las-sombrillas-0.

[152] See, for example, Vendrell's comments on earlier tenors in his memoir *El mestre Millet i jo: Memòries* (Barcelona: Aymà, 1953), 229.

younger singers had operatic leanings, for some trained as opera singers at conservatoires (e.g., Felisa Herrero and Mary Isaura), while others received scholarships to study in Italy (e.g., Cora Raga and Marcos Redondo) and began their opera careers there before returning to Spain.

An important difference between these singers and those of previous generations is that general musicianship constituted a more prominent role in the younger singers' training. Many of them read notation fluently, which was not always the case with their predecessors, who usually had to learn on the job.[153] Vendrell himself insisted that all singers must be able to read music.[154] Composers were well aware of this shift and its implications for performance practice. They were not only writing some vocally demanding music, often influenced by operetta and verismo, but also producing scores that were more detailed in terms of expressivity.

Central to this discussion, slurs were often used to indicate pairs of notes between which portamento was recommended. The absence of portamento in such instances in period recordings, however, suggests that such slurs were seen as encouragements, not mandates, and were ultimately optional. This also implies that fidelity to the score, while increasingly important, still carried with it a significant degree of flexibility.

Composers often ran their own production companies and therefore worked closely with singers. They would have seen and heard first hand how new expressive codes were developing, how they interfaced with existing conventions regarding portamento and how a new generation of singers was balancing the two approaches. They would also have had ample opportunity to reflect on how to translate these practices into notation, but always with the awareness that singers could (and often would) still resort to their previous approaches to interpretation when it came to departing from what appeared on the page. *Zarzuela* singers of the 1920s and 1930s, it becomes clear, were highly skilled professionals. They were musically literate and keenly aware of unwritten conventions. Their use of recording technologies to benefit their careers and to document their unique performance practices, including portamento, was unprecedented in the genre.

Zarzuela and *Zarzuela* Recordings during and after the Spanish Civil War, 1936–1953

The Spanish Civil War (1936–1939) disrupted musical life in Spain in profound ways. Many leaders of the musical avant-garde active in the 1920s and 1930s,

---

[153] Vendrell, *El mestre Millet i jo*, 71; Gómez Manzanares, *Felisa Herrero*, 18–19.

[154] Vendrell, *El cant*, 41.

such as Salvador Bacarisse and Rodolfo Halffter, were forced into exile. This precipitated a leadership crisis in the first few months of the war, one that forced the veteran composer Joaquín Turina into the position of Comisario de Música. Good orchestral conductors were seen as few and far between, a dilemma that constituted a serious obstacle to the continuation of musical life.[155] In the realm of *zarzuela*, however, the disruption was felt to a lesser extent.

During the war, *zarzuela* continued to be performed extensively by both Republicans and Nationalists, which is a testament to how *zarzuela* could resonate among a range of national identity concerns, regardless of specific ideology. Performances typically relied on the established repertoire and not on new works.[156] On both sides of the political divide, companies needed to be able to quickly mount productions that would both be financially solvent and improve public morale.

Proof of how popular *zarzuela* was on the Republican side is the fact that some of its cities nationalized their theatres to keep them going. Singers and in fact all theatrical workers were paid a modest salary from the government. Under this system, a *primera tiple* would often earn the same as a driver. In Madrid, which remained in the hands of the Republicans until the final days of the war, numerous *beneficio* performances were organized with the aim of collecting donations for various pro-Republican causes. Musical life in Madrid was fast-paced and often chaotic. In order to boost attendance, performances were often advertised as featuring certain very popular singers, who would then fail to appear. Sometimes, the same singer was advertised as performing in two different theatres on the same day at the same time.[157] While such announcements prove the unreliability of individual press reports, they collectively show that *zarzuela* remained extremely popular with audiences in Republican Madrid. *Zarzuelas* flourished alongside lighter genres with similar popular appeal, such as *revistas*. In fact, *zarzuelas* and *revistas* sometimes appeared on the same programme.[158]

On the Nationalist side, the singers Emili Vendrell, Hipólito Lázaro and Marcos Redondo, all of whom were well established in the *zarzuela* scene, found themselves in Barcelona when the theatres there fell under the control of the anarchist trade union CNT (Confederación Nacional de Trabajadores). They were given a salary of fifteen *pesetas* per performance (in peacetime, they could earn as much as one thousand[159]) and were having to sing physically and

---

[155] Eva Moreda Rodríguez, *Music Criticism and Music Critics in Early Francoist Spain* (New York: Oxford University Press, 2016), 43.

[156] 'Vida musical', *El pensamiento alavés*, 7 January 1939.

[157] Gómez Manzanares, *Felisa Herrero*, 186.

[158] R. Garea, 'Saloncillo', *ABC*, 10 October 1937.

[159] Lázaro, *El libro de mi vida*, 585; Emili Vendrell Jr, *El meu pare* (Barcelona: Toray, 1965), 52; see also Marcos Redondo, *Un hombre que se va* (Barcelona: Planeta, 1973), 226. Redondo and

vocally demanding runs in Barcelona, in various towns throughout Catalonia and on occasional international tours.[160] Such activities, organized by the Catalan government, were designed to keep morale high on the home front. So that companies could cope with the massive demand for performances, repertoires were pared down to a small number of extremely popular works, both old and more recent. These included *Marina, Doña Francisquita, La rosa del azafrán, La tabernera del puerto, La del manojo de rosas, Bohemios, El dúo de la Africana* and *El cabo primero.*[161] At the same time, the Catalan government was showing interest in revitalizing to a certain extent the more prestigious Spanish operatic repertoire through performances of José María Usandizaga's *Las golondrinas,*[162] Tomás Bretón's *La Dolores*, Enrique Granados's *María del Carmen* and Manuel de Falla's *La vida breve.*[163] Furthermore, the Nationalists reconceptualized the social role of radio and for the first time in Spanish history radio was being used as a propaganda tool. This led to *zarzuela* often being featured on the leisure broadcasts of Radio Nacional, alongside opera, Spanish art music and standard classical repertoire.

Central to the present discussion, very few, if any, new recordings of *zarzuela* were made by either side. While there certainly would have been constraints to producing such recordings, particularly in terms of international circulation, it is likely that both Nationalists and Republicans were sceptical as to recordings' potential value as propaganda. Live performances would have no doubt provided a sense of community among those in the audience who were coming together in the same physical place and listening to live radio broadcasts would have engendered a sense of connection among those listening to the same programme at the same time all over Spain, an 'imagined community', to use Benedict Anderson's term.[164] Recordings, however, because they lacked the live quality that could bring people together, might have been regarded as less

---

Lázaro, along with María Espinalt and Enrique Borrás, managed to obtain a pay rise from the CNT in June 1937 on account of their star status; see Redondo, *Un hombre que se va*, 226.

[160] For example, Vendrell toured France, Czechoslovakia, Belgium and Switzerland in June to November 1937 (Vendrell Jr, *El meu pare*, 52).

[161] Lázaro was ideologically right wing and managed to escape Barcelona for Latin America after having been granted leave by the president of the Spanish Republic, Juan Negrín (Lázaro, *El libro de mi vida*, 581–582; Redondo, *Un hombre que se va*, 215).

[162] *Las golondrinas* was first performed as a *zarzuela* in 1914 and subsequently adapted as an opera by Usandizaga's brother, Ramón, and premiered as such at the Teatro del Liceu.

[163] Isabel Ferrer Senabre, 'Ruperto Chapí y la zarzuela: Ambivalencias musicales en la Guerra Civil Española', in Víctor Sánchez Sánchez, Javier Suárez Pajares and Vicente Galbis López, eds., *Ruperto Chapí: Nuevas perspectivas* (Valencia: Institut Valencià de la Música, 2012), vol. 2, 191–207, especially 195–97.

[164] Benedict Anderson, *Imagined Communities: Reflections on the Origin and Spread of Nationalism* (London: Verso, 1983; 2nd ed., London: Verso, 2006).

useful for identity-building purposes in a time of war. The act of solitary listening that had been developing in previous decades had lost its foothold.

After the Civil War ended in 1939, the *zarzuela* scene re-established itself relatively quickly. Some companies toured the provinces while others settled in the main theatres in Madrid and Barcelona. Signs were emerging, however, that the genre was losing some of its energy as a living art form. Companies were becoming increasingly reliant on past repertoire and the lack of sufficient financial funding and artistic vision were being felt. Productions were all too often regarded as lacklustre and poorly rehearsed.[165] Some of this can be attributed to the uncertainty in which the music profession had to operate in post-war times (as was also the case for other art forms). Younger audiences were choosing other types of entertainment such as the cinema and new generations of composers were no longer interested in creating *zarzuelas*, particularly since other, more lucrative possibilities were emerging in other areas of popular music.

Although live performances of *zarzuela* resumed after the war ended, recordings did not. This likely had to do with the lack of vigour of the *zarzuela* scene on stage and the absence of significant technological innovations that could have sparked either a renewed interest in recorded music or a shift in performance practices. While the continuous production of recordings from 1900 to 1936 (sometimes with the same singer recording the same number several times within a few years[166]) often offers crucial evidence to show how certain performance practices gradually changed, for the period from 1936 to 1953, we are, to a great extent, in the dark.

Some important recordings were made in the post-Civil War years, to be sure. These include composer Pablo Sorozábal conducting selections from his successful, yet controversial *zarzuela La tabernera del puerto*[167] in 1943. Evidence from such recordings suggests continuity rather than drastic change in the use of portamento. For example, in 'terceto cómico', the comic characters, performed by the singers Enriqueta Serrano (as Antigua) and Manuel Alares (as Chinchorro)

---

[165] 'Teatros', *Hoja oficial del lunes*, 8 May 1944.

[166] For example, Lucrecia Arana's recordings of romanzas from *La viejecita* and *Gigantes y cabezudos*.

[167] *La tabernera del puerto* had its premiere in April 1936 (three months before the start of the Civil War) and was recorded for the first time shortly thereafter. It was performed in Spain throughout the 1940s and became a great audience success. However, Sorozábal's support for the Republic during the war attracted negative criticism toward the work. An article in 1940 ('*La tabernera del puerto*', *Diario de Burgos*, 28 May 1940) described it as musically excellent but morally suspect (likely because of the willingness of the two main characters to engage in drug trafficking to secure a future for themselves). In the same year, an organised clique booed a performance in Madrid, accusing Sorozábal of being a Republican (Pablo Sorozábal, *Mi vida, mi obra* (Madrid: Fundación Banco Exterior, 1986), 237–242).

employ portamento of the comic variety described above, while the more serious character Marola, performed by Pepita Embil, does not.[168]

Zarzuela on Long-Play (LP) Records, 1953–1958

The next significant milestone in the history of *zarzuela* recording did not arrive until the 1950s, following the introduction of the long-play 33 rpm record by Columbia in 1948. This technology made it possible to record complete *zarzuelas* for the first time. From 1953 onwards, several conductors and labels undertook full recordings of *zarzuelas*. These were made mostly through a series of small Spanish labels (e.g., Hispavox, Alhambra) that were affiliated with multinationals. The recordings were intended primarily for the local market in Spain, although some full-length recordings were also made in the Americas for Spanish-speaking audiences in the Western hemisphere.[169] Since new works were rare, these recordings focused mainly on established repertoire. Some especially popular *zarzuelas* were recorded multiple times within a short period. For example, no less than three recordings of *Gigantes y cabezudos* appeared in 1954 in what seems to have been a race to conquer a growing domestic market.[170] Other *zarzuelas*, such as *El rey que rabió*, were being recorded for the first time since the early 1930s.[171]

Significantly, this revival of *zarzuela* recordings coincided with what can be termed the death of *zarzuela* on stage. It was no longer a thriving theatrical genre characterized by the creation and production of new works. Neither of the two most popular living *zarzuela* composers at the time, Pablo Sorozábal and Federico Moreno Torroba, were producing new works to the same degree as

---

[168] Pepita Embil, Enriqueta Serrano, Manuel Alares and Pablo Sorozábal, 'Terceto cómico', from *La tabernera del puerto,* by Pablo Sorozabal, recorded by Columbia in 1943, matrix no. C 5657, no digitization available.

[169] For example, in Cuba, Martha Pérez, Francisco Naya, Maruja González, Enrique Cámara and Gonzalo Roig, *Luisa Fernanda,* by Federico Moreno Torroba, recorded for Soria Series, ca. 1950; and Blanca Varela, Miguel de Grandy, Mario Martínez Casado, María Márquez and Gonzalo Roig, *La parranda,* by Francisco Alonso, recorded for unknown label, 1961. Roig also recorded Cuban *zarzuela* around the same time.

[170] Ataúlfo Argenta (conductor), *Gigantes y cabezudos*, by Manuel Fernández Caballero, recorded in 1954 for Alhambra, issue no. MCC 30009; Enrique Ribó (conductor), *Gigantes y cabezudos*, by Manuel Fernández Caballero, recorded in 1954 for Odeón, issue no. Regal 33LCX 117; and Daniel Montorio and Enrique Navarro (conductors), *Gigantes y cabezudos*, by Manuel Fernández Caballero, recorded in 1954 for Hispavox, issue no. Montilla: FM-19.

[171] In 1931, two different collections of the main numbers of the work were released: Mary Isaura, Amparo Albiach, Enrique Parra, Ángel de León, Ignacio Cornadó, Pedro Vidal and Concordio Gelabert, numbers from *El rey que rabió*, by Ruperto Chapí, recorded for Gramophone in 1931; and Ángeles Ottein, Sara Fenor, Manuel Alba, Manuel Gorgé, José Palomo, Eduardo Marcén and Modesto Romero, numbers from *El rey que rabió*, by Ruperto Chapí, recorded for Odeón in 1931.

they had in the past and neither was enjoying the same level of success as had been the case in the 1930s.

Zarzuela's new home turned out to be the LP record. Several conductors were central to this revival of classic *zarzuela* in the recording studio. Especially important were Ataúlfo Argenta, Daniel Montorio, Enrique Navarro, Rafael Ferrer and Ricardo Estevarena as well as the previously mentioned composer-conductors Sorozábal and Moreno Torroba. In the cases of Sorozábal and Moreno Torroba, they mainly recorded LPs of their own *zarzuelas*, just as they had done in the 1930s with individual *zarzuela* numbers.

It was Argenta, more than anyone else, who restored the dignity of *zarzuela* by taking it into homes throughout Spain and indeed around the world at a time during which the genre's popularity on stage was increasingly in decline. A key figure in the histories of *zarzuela* and post-Civil War Spanish musical life, Argenta made *zarzuela* a respectable genre on par with the classical canon. When critically examining his invaluable contribution to *zarzuela*, however, we must bear in mind that his contemporaries mythologized him and his achievements to a considerable degree. His untimely death in 1958 at the age of forty-four no doubt contributed significantly to his legendary status.

An anecdote from the journalist and critic Antonio Fernández-Cid is particularly illustrative of how Argenta's reputation as a champion of *zarzuela* was built. Fernández-Cid claimed that Argenta often told his musicians to perform the accompaniment to the dialogue between Don Sebastián and Don Hilarión in *La verbena de la Paloma* with the same care and attention as when they were playing Mozart.[172] *Zarzuela*, in his estimation, was equal to *opera buffa* as a musical-dramatic genre. Argenta's supporters also routinely commented on his loyalty to the notated score as fundamental to his efforts as a renovator of *zarzuela*. He was said to have brought the genre in line with practices of strict adherence to the score typical of the classical canon.[173]

Key to Argenta's reputation was the fact that he, unlike many other conductors recording *zarzuela* during these years,[174] had achieved considerable success both in Spain and abroad conducting the standard orchestral repertoire. Several

---

[172] Antonio Fernández-Cid, *Ataúlfo Argenta* (Santander: Servicio de Publicaciones de la Universidad de Cantabria, 2003), 201.

[173] Rafael Frühbeck de Burgos, quoted in Alberto González Lapuente and Alberto Honrado Pinilla, 'Coloquio: Zarzuela e interpretación: Origen y destino', in Alberto González Lapuente and Alberto Honrado Pinilla, eds., *Horizontes de la zarzuela* (Madrid: Fundación Jacinto e Inocencio Guerrero, 2014), 141–159, especially 143. Frühbeck de Burgos succeeded Argenta as conductor of the Orquesta Nacional de España.

[174] Sorozábal sometimes appeared as an orchestral conductor in Francoist Spain, for example as guest conductor for the Orquesta Filarmónica de Madrid. Unlike Argenta, conducting was not his main occupation and he did not achieve the same level of international recognition as Argenta. Rafael Ferrer was also active as a conductor of regional orchestras in Spain.

biographers claim this as proof that Argenta was truly committed to *zarzuela* and was even happy to let his international orchestral conducting career take second seat to his work in *zarzuela*. He intentionally chose *zarzuela* rather than being pushed into it because of a lack of other options.[175]

Argenta's status as a champion of *zarzuela* was also due to his choice of repertoire. In six years, from 1953 to 1958, Argenta recorded around sixty *zarzuelas*, an astonishing number.[176] The sheer quantity of his output as well as his repertoire choices reflect his desire to establish a *zarzuela* canon at a time when the genre was not teeming with new works. Argenta's canon was decidedly composer-centric, with eleven composers taking up almost ninety percent of the list. This explains why his discography includes, besides the hugely popular pieces that had been in the repertoire since the late nineteenth century, several relatively obscure works by otherwise well-known composers, such as Chueca (*El chaleco blanco*) and Chapí (*La patria chica*).

In Argenta's hands, the history of *zarzuela* thus became a list of composers and works, similar to the way that Western classical music was being canonized at the time. The early history of modern *zarzuela* – up to the birth of *género chico* in 1880 – is represented in Argenta's recordings by three *zarzuelas grandes* from the composer Asenjo Barbieri, two of which, *Jugar con fuego* and *Los diamantes de la corona*, had rarely been heard either live or on recordings during the previous decades. The third work, *El barberillo de Lavapiés*, on the other hand, was an established classic, even though it was not performed all that often. These three recordings suggest that Argenta was striving, at least somewhat, to reclaim a golden age of *zarzuela* that modern audiences did not know particularly well. His efforts in this regard were limited, for he did not record any works by other *zarzuela grande* pioneers of the time,

---

[175] Fernández-Cid, *Ataúlfo Argenta*, 203; José Montero Alonso, *Ataúlfo Argenta* (Santander: La Moderna, 1959), clxxxv; Jacinto Molina, *Ataúlfo Argenta: Un año de ausencia* (San Sebastián: Fábrica de Discos Columbia, 1959), 3.

[176] Listed by composer: Francisco Alonso (*La parranda*), Francisco Asenjo Barbieri (*Jugar con fuego, Los diamantes de la corona, El barberillo de Lavapiés*), Tomás Bretón (*La verbena de la Paloma*), Ruperto Chapí (*La tempestad, El tambor de granaderos, El barquillero, Música clásica, La patria chica, El puñao de rosas, El rey que rabió*), Federico Chueca (*Agua, azucarillos y aguardiente, La alegría de la huerta, El chaleco blanco, La gran vía*), Manuel Fernández Caballero (*El dúo de la Africana, La viejecita, El cabo primero, Gigantes y cabezudos*), Gerónimo Giménez (*El baile de Luis Alonso, La boda de Luis Alonso*), Jacinto Guerrero (*Los gavilanes, La alsaciana*), Jesús Guridi (*El caserío*), Vicente Lleó (*La corte de Faraón*), Pablo Luna (*Molinos de viento, La chula de Pontevedra, El asombro de Damasco, Los cadetes de la reina, El niño judío*), Tomás López Torregrosa (*La fiesta de San Antón, El santo de la Isidra*), Giuseppe Mazza, arranged by Vicente Lleó (*El maestro campanone*), Rafael Millán Picazo (*La dogaresa*), Federico Moreno Torroba (*Luisa Fernanda*), Manuel Penella (*Don Gil de Alcalá*), José Serrano (*La reina mora, Los de Aragón, La dolorosa, Alma de Dios, La canción del olvido, Los claveles, Moros y Cristianos*), Reveriano Soutullo and Juan Vert (*La del soto del parral, El último romántico*) and Amadeo Vives (*Bohemios, Doña Francisquita, Maruxa*).

such as Joaquín Gaztambide, Pedro Marqués, Cristóbal Oudrid or Tomás Bretón (in his pre-*La verbena de la Paloma* endeavours).

Argenta also made numerous recordings of *género chico*. In doing so, he clearly embraced the views that some in intellectual circles had been expressing since the 1910s:[177] *género chico*, even though light-hearted and incidental in some ways, featured some excellent music and performed an embodiment of Spanish identity. As was to be expected, Argenta recorded universally successful works that had remained in the repertoire practically since their premieres (e.g., *La revoltosa*, *La verbena de la Paloma* and *La Gran Vía*) as well as others that had achieved considerable success in their time but then fell in popularity (e.g., *El barberillo de Lavapiés* and *El juramento*). Argenta therefore provided listening audiences with a broader and more nuanced picture of *género chico* than what could have been seen on stage.

While it would be anachronistically misleading to speak of a commitment to historical performance practice in Argenta's recordings of the earliest *zarzuelas*, an examination of portamento in his recordings can provide further insights into the conductor's ambition to reshape *zarzuela*'s past in terms of its present. *Zarzuelas* such as *La viejecita* and *Doña Francisquita* had been regularly recorded since their premieres, which allows us to hear a continuum in terms of their performance practices. Others, like *El rey que rabió* and *La verbena de la Paloma*, whose popularity waxed and waned, were also recorded numerous times over the years. These recordings provide us with aural snapshots through which we can hear and understand how the approach to some numbers or roles changed over time.[178]

This is not the case with *El barberillo de Lavapiés*, however. After the 1902 recording of the romanza 'Canción de Paloma' discussed earlier, *the zarzuela* was not recorded to any significant degree for about fifty years.[179] It only

---

[177]   Conrado del Campo, 'Sobre la situación actual de la música española', *Revista musical hispanoamericana* 1 (1914), 2–4; Juan Borrás de Palau, 'Sobre la ópera nacional', *Revista musical hispanoamericana* 9 (1914), 4–5; Eduardo López Chavarri, 'Teatro y música nacional', *Revista musical hispanoamericana* 16 (1915), 3; Rogelio Villar, 'Divagaciones sobre el nacionalismo musical y los compositores españoles', *Revista musical hispanoamericana* 20 (1915), 2–5; Rogelio Villar, 'A mis amigos de la Sociedad Nacional', *Revista musical hispanoamericana* 1 [third season] (1916), 4–6.

[178]   For example, the role of Julián in *La verbena de la Paloma*, which I have discussed elsewhere (Moreda Rodríguez, 'Singing and Speaking in Early Twentieth-Century *Zarzuela*', 43–47).

[179]   Rafael Bezares and Lolita Escalona, 'Dúo-Tirana', by Francisco Asenjo Barbieri, recorded by Odeón in 1905, matrix no. XS 673, http://bdh.bne.es/bnesearch/detalle/bdh0000149852 (Cara A); Srta. Colombini, 'El barberillo de Lavapiés: Canción de paloma', by Francisco Asenjo Barbieri, recorded by Gramophone in 1905, matrix no. 5287; Srta. Colombini and Sr. Claro Moreno, 'El barberillo de Lavapiés: Dúo', by Francico Asenjo Barbieri, recorded by Gramophone in 1905, matrix no. 5289; Sr. Ortiz, 'El barberillo de Lavapiés', by Francisco Asenjo Barbieri, recorded by Gramophone in 1905, matrix no. 5296; Srta. Colombini, Sr. Ortiz, Sr. Claro Moreno, 'El barberillo de Lavapiés – Caleseras', by Francisco Asenjo Barbieri,

y pen - sar   mu - choen tu   cuer - po chi - qui - to, tu la - bio bo

Figure 10 'Dúo-tirana' from *El barberillo de Lavapiés*, bars 49–51, as
performed in the 1956 Hispavox recording conducted by Enrique Navarro

Ti - ra - naahí   va

Figure 11 'Dúo-tirana' from *El barberillo de Lavapiés*, bars 111–12, as
performed in the 1956 Hispavox recording conducted by Enrique Navarro

Yo   sir-voal   con - de

Figure 12 Tercet from *El barberillo de Lavapiés*, bars 16–17, as performed in
the 1955 Alhambra recording conducted by Ataúlfo Argenta

y   lle-var   deo - ro   re-ple-toel bol - si - llo

Figure 13 'Dúo-tirana' from *El barberillo de Lavapiés*, bars 81–82, as
performed in the 1955 Alhambra recording conducted by Ataúlfo Argenta

returned to the studio in the 1950s with Argenta and his contemporaries.
Argenta's recording was released in 1955[180] and another, conducted by
Enrique Navarro, appeared the following year.[181] The uses of portamento in
these recordings yields several telling insights (see Figures 10–13).

These examples are really not that different in their use of portamento
conventions from other recordings discussed in this Element, particularly

recorded by Gramophone in 1905, matrix no. 5296; Sr. Navarro, 'El barberillo de Lavapiés', by
Francisco Asenjo Barbieri, recorded by Gramophone in 1907, matrix no. 6245. No digitizations
of the gramophone records are available.

[180] Ana María Olaria, Teresa Berganza, Carlos Munguía, Gerardo Monreal, Ataúlfo Argenta, *El
barberillo de Lavapiés*, by Francisco Asenjo Barbieri, recorded for Alhambra in 1955, issue no.
SMGE 80316.

[181] Dolores Pérez, Isabel Garcisanz, Santiago Ramalle, Tino Moro, Ramón Alonso, Juan Pascual,
Enrique Navarro, *El barberillo de Lavapiés*, by Francisco Asenjo Barbieri, recorded for
Hispavox in 1956, issue no. Montilla FM-48.

those following the arrival of electrical recordings. Expressive portamento was applied mainly on larger descending intervals at the ends of phrases, though less often than on the earlier cylinder recordings. We can therefore speak of a performance tradition that was part reconstruction and part invention, with Argenta and his singers not aiming so much to replicate how *El barberillo* would have been performed in the 1880s – such an approach would be have been largely unthought of at the time – but rather to perform the *zarzuela* in a way that fit within the genre's expressive codes as they were understood in the 1950s. On the other hand, the extensive use of portamento in Argenta's recordings, as well as other performance decisions such as frequent tempo modifications, calls into question his reputation for always sticking to the score. Such liberties are often heard in other *zarzuela* (and opera) recordings from the decade and are not unique to Argenta's approach to *zarzuela*.

None of the singers who sang on these LP recordings completely broke away from past performance practices while they were making their own marks on what might be considered to constitute a *zarzuela* aesthetic at the time. Some of these singers came from the first generation to take full advantage of electrical recording, such as Marcos Redondo (who in 1954 recorded a new *Luisa Fernanda* for Hispavox conducted by its composer, Moreno Torroba)[182] and Sélica Pérez Carpio (who played the supporting role of Gorgonia in Argenta's recording of *La revoltosa*).[183] In recordings of romanzas from *Doña Francisquita* conducted by Rafael Ferrer in 1953[184] and Argenta in 1954,[185] the use of portamento maps remarkably well to what has been discussed in this Element so far. Since *Doña Francisquita* never left the repertoire, it is likely that Emili Vendrell, who kept singing Fernando until his retirement in 1953, provided such a strong link with past portamento traditions that they almost became conventions. The role of such singers in ensuring a continuity in performance practice was significant, for through

---

[182] Rosario Gómez, Pablo Civil, Lolita Torrentó, Marcos Redondo and Federico Moreno Torroba, *Luisa Fernanda*, by Federico Moreno Torroba, recorded for Hispavox in 1954, issue no. Regal 33LCX 103.

[183] Ana María Iriarte, Inés Rivadeneira, Sélica Pérez Carpio, Manuel Ausensi, Miguel Ligero, Rafael López Somoza, Perecito and Ataúlfo Argenta, *La revoltosa*, by Ruperto Chapí, recorded for Alhambra in 1953, issue no. MCC 30001.

[184] Lolita Torrentó, Pablo Civil, Rosario Gómez, Juan José Márquez and Rafael Ferrer, several numbers from *Doña Francisquita*, by Amadeo Vives, recorded for Odeón in 1954, http://bdh .bne.es/bnesearch/detalle/bdh0000176172, matrix nos. CKX 3760, CKX 3746, CKX 3747, CKX 3748, CKX 3749, CKX 3750, CKX 3751, CKX 3752, CKX 3753, CKX 3754, CKX 3755, CKX 3756, CKX 3757, CKX 3758.

[185] María de los Ángeles Morales, Carlos Munguía, Ana María Iriarte, Julio Uribe and Ataúlfo Argenta, *Doña Francisquita*, by Amadeo Vives, recorded for Alhambra in 1954, issue no. MCC 30014 and MCC 30015.

their LP recordings they provide aural glimpses of what little we know about *zarzuela* performances practices in the years following the Spanish Civil War. Most of the singers we hear in 1950s LPs of *zarzuelas*, however, were newer to the scene. Argenta preferred to work with the same small group of singers for multiple recordings: Ana María Iriarte, Toñy Rosado, Inés Rivadeneira, Manuel Ausensi and Carlos Munguía. These were all singers with whom he had recently worked on stage.[186] All of them were at the beginning of their careers and many, like Iriarte, were recent conservatory graduates, with minimal or no professional stage experience. This careful choice of singers became a key feature of Argenta's reputation as a renovator of *zarzuela*. His various biographers collectively agree that Argenta did not want to hire singers who had acquired bad habits and settled for substandard singing technique from years of inadequate, rushed rehearsals and working with poor conductors.[187] These biographies do not state exactly what these bad habits and techniques were, however. Not every older singer who recorded on LPs fit this description, as we can hear in recordings by Vendrell, Redondo, Pérez Carpio, Raga and others.

Several of the younger singers heard on *zarzuela* LPs from the 1950s also had careers in opera, such as Pablo Civil and Luis Sagi-Vela, the latter the son of noted *zarzuela* performers Emilio Sagi Barba and Luisa Vela. Some would soon establish international careers, as was the case with Alfredo Kraus, Teresa Berganza and Pilar Lorengar.

These younger singers had more systematic classical training than those from previous generations, which to a great extent translated into the continuation of certain performance practices, including the use of portamento. The change in aesthetics when compared to earlier decades of recorded technologies is perhaps most obvious, though, in the increasingly consistent use of vibrato. Still, some remnants of past performance practices lived on, as is revealed in the 1956 Hispavox recording of *Luisa Fernanda* conducted by Enrique Estela.[188] Playing the role of Duquesa Carolina, Natalia Lombay's vibrato is very wide in the upper range, but her middle and low registers reflect the low soft palate placement and chest dominant delivery reminiscent of earlier eras.

When compared with previous decades, portamento technique in the 1950s became more uniform across *zarzuela grande* and *género chico*. There are also

---

[186] Argenta's *zarzuela* career started in 1951, when he conducted a short season of *zarzuela* (*La verbena de la Paloma*, *La Revoltosa* and *Agua, azucarillos y aguardiente*) in Madrid. Some of Argenta's flagship singers performed in this inaugural season; see Fernández-Cid, *Ataúlfo Argenta*, 197–199 and Montero Alonso, *Ataúlfo Argenta*, clxxxv.

[187] Fernández-Cid, *Ataúlfo Argenta*, 197–200.

[188] Dolores Pérez, Natalia Lombay, Miguel Sierra, Luis Sagi-Vela and Enrique Estela, *Luisa Fernanda*, by Federico Moreno Torroba, recorded for Hispavox in 1956, issue no. Montilla: FM-67, digitization not available.

hints that determining when portamento would be used had also become more standardized. For example, the portamento-legatos on intervals of a second, as discussed earlier, continued to be standard practice. Expressive portamento appears mostly on descending fourths and fifths (and to a much lesser extent, on octaves and thirds), normally at the end of a phrase (though sometimes in the middle) and usually on a word the performer may have wanted to emphasize. Improvements in recording technologies as well as in the vocal training of singers allows us to hear greater nuances than had been the case previously. This confirms that the stylistic trends heard in pre-Spanish Civil War recordings continued into the 1950s. While each singer's approach to executing portamento certainly remained an individual choice, portamento in general was now being performed quickly rather than slowly and in a more understated way than was the case in the very early recordings. Overall, this practice follows contemporary developments in other genres while resonating more readily with present-day tastes and sensibilities.

Conclusion

The plethora of studies that make use of early recordings as sources for performance practice have given us much more knowledge now than we had ten or twenty years ago about *how* performing styles (for specific instruments, genres or geographies) changed over the first decades of the twentieth century. Tackling the question of *why* performing styles change, however, is more challenging and is not always explicitly addressed in such studies. Beyond attributing shifts to nebulous matters of taste, some authors attempt to offer answers. Mark Katz, as discussed earlier, coined 'phonograph effect' as a catch-all term to explain how recording technologies influenced the way musicians performed in live situations[189] and Daniel Leech-Wilkinson hypothesizes that changes in performance practices towards the middle of the twentieth century might have been motivated by societies becoming more self-conscious and cynical after the Second World War.[190] Interestingly, Katz and Leech-Wilkinson's answers fall on almost opposite ends of the spectrum: from the eminently practical, logistical and mechanical to the overwhelmingly abstract.

In this Element, I have attempted to illustrate how early recordings can be used not only to locate and describe change but also to explain how and why it came about. My task has been considerably facilitated by *zarzuela* being primarily, though not exclusively, composed and recorded in one specific place: Spain. The study of *zarzuela*, though, truly calls for transnational

---

[189] Katz, *Capturing Sound*, 102.
[190] Leech-Wilkinson, 'Portamento and Musical Meaning', 250.

approaches. It was shaped throughout its history through dialogues with musics from elsewhere and it circulated in Spanish-speaking countries outside Spain. *Zarzuela*'s production and consumption through the medium of recordings, however, was more localized than was the case for, say, opera and orchestral music (with some notable exceptions). This geographical limitation has made it easier to identify and pin down the various contexts and spheres likely to have influenced the performance practices associated with portamento.

These practices start with the recording technologies themselves in terms of both their technological development over time and the commercial practices they engendered. Such shifts in turn resulted in new ways of consuming and listening to music and in new discourses on music and sound. Also important were changes in the *zarzuela* scene itself. With some of them, such as the working structure of the music profession and the training of singers, it might be relatively simple to establish cause-and-effect relationships; such matters, however, are often closely connected to broader issues concerning the social status of *zarzuela* at any given point in time and its perceived connections to national identity.

The challenge is to determine the extent to which such factors might be heard in recordings. There is a real danger to quasi-mechanistically relate every performance element to a contextual development. Such actions risk losing sight of key aspects of these recordings and the performances they capture. Beyond performance conventions and technological constraints, there was still ample room for personal preference and for the randomness that is inherent in the interactions between musicians and recording technologies. Taken together, these factors tend to delimit a range of expressive possibilities for portamento rather than establishing a set of hard and fast rules. What we hear in these recordings are *some* of these expressive possibilities. Especially for the earlier years, it is easy to see how the picture remains incomplete, but a comparison of recordings, as well as consideration of their cultural and social circumstances, can certainly help us make sense of practices that on first hearing might sound hybridized, changeable and multifarious.

One of the key factors in this Element has been the notion that *zarzuela*'s requirements and priorities were dominated to a considerable extent by the need to convey text expressively. The centrality of language powerfully connects portamento performance practices in *zarzuela* with those in other genres. Portamento has often been described as an attempt to translate aspects of speech into singing and the present study offers a more detailed look into how this happened in the realm of *zarzuela*.

Secondary Sources

Alonso, Celsa. 'Ruperto Chapí: Música, pragmatismo y heterodoxia'. In *Ruperto Chapí: Nuevas perspectivas*, edited by Víctor Sánchez Sánchez, Javier Suárez Pajares and Vicente Galbis López, 23–51. Valencia: Institut Valencià de la Música, 2012.

Arca Caldas, Olimpio. *Unha voz . . . Mary Isaura*. A Estrada: Asociación Fillos e Amigos da Estrada, 2001.

Ashby, Arved. *Absolute Music, Mechanical Reproduction*. Oakland, CA: University of California Press, 2010.

Bolig, John R. *The Victor Discography: Green, Blue, and Purple Labels (1910–1926)*. Denver, CO: Mainspring Press, 2006.

Brandenberger, Tobias and Antje Dreyer, eds. *La zarzuela y sus caminos: Del siglo XVII a la actualidad*. Berlin: Lit, 2016.

Casares Rodicio, Emilio. *Francisco Asenjo Barbieri: El hombre y el creador*. Madrid: Editorial Complutense, 1994.

'Voz'. *Diccionario de la zarzuela en España e Hispanoamérica*, vol. 2, edited by Emilio Casares Rodicio, 941–944. Madrid: Instituto Complutense de Ciencias Musicales, 2006.

editor. *Diccionario de la zarzuela en España e Hispanoamérica*. 2 vols. Madrid: Instituto Complutense de Ciencias Musicales, 2006.

Cortizo, María Encina. *Emilio Arrieta: De la ópera a la zarzuela*. Madrid: Instituto Complutense de Ciencias Musicales, 1998.

Cotarelo y Mori, Emilio. *Historia de la zarzuela*. Madrid: Instituto Complutense de Ciencias Musicales, 2001.

Deleito y Piñuela, José. *Origen y apogeo del 'género chico'*. Madrid: Revista de Occidente, 1949.

Denning, Michael. *Noise Uprising: The Audiopolitics of a World Musical Revolution*. London: Verso Books, 2015.

Encabo, Enrique. *Música y nacionalismos en España*. Barcelona: Erasmus, 2006.

Feaster, Patrick. '"Rise and Obey the Command": Performative Fidelity and the Exercise of Phonographic Power'. *Journal of Popular Music Studies* 24, no. 3 (2012): 357–395.

Fernández-Cid, Antonio. *Ataúlfo Argenta*. Santander: Servicio de Publicaciones de la Universidad de Cantabria, 2003.

Ferrer Senabre, Isabel. 'Ruperto Chapí y la zarzuela: Ambivalencias musicales en la Guerra Civil Española'. In *Ruperto Chapí: Nuevas perspectivas*, vol. 2, edited by Víctor Sánchez Sánchez, Javier Suárez Pajares and Vicente Galbis López, 191–207. Valencia: Institut Valencià de la Música, 2012.

Freitas, Roger. 'Towards a Verdian Ideal of Singing: Emancipation from Modern Orthodoxy'. *Journal of the Royal Musical Association* 127, no. 2 (2002): 226–257.

García Torres, Andrea. 'El teatro lírico como género difusor de las ideologías dominantes en torno a la Guerra de África (1859–1860)'. *Anuario Musical* 72 (2017): 191–208.

Gauß, Stefan. 'Listening to the Horn: On the Cultural History of the Phonograph and the Gramophone'. In *Sounds of Modern History: Auditory Cultures in 19th- and 20th-Century Europe*, edited by Daniel Morat, 71–100. Oxford: Berghahn, 2014.

Gentili, Barbara. 'The Changing Aesthetics of Vocal Registration in the Age of "Verismo"'. *Music and Letters* 102, no. 1 (2020): 54–79.

Gómez Manzanares, Pedro. *Felisa Herrero: Musa de la zarzuela*. Madrid: Cultiva Libros, 2011.

González Lapuente, Alberto and Alberto Honrado Pinilla. 'Coloquio: Zarzuela e interpretación: Origen y destino'. In *Horizontes de la zarzuela*, edited by Alberto González Lapuente and Alberto Honrado Pinilla, *please give page numbers*. Madrid: Fundación Jacinto e Inocencio Guerrero, 2014.

González Peña, María Luz, Javier Suárez-Pajares and Julio Arce Bueno. *Mujeres de la escena 1900–1940*. Madrid: SGAE, 1996.

Harney, Lucy D. 'Controlling Resistance, Resisting Control: The *género chico* and the Dynamics of Mass Entertainment in Late Nineteenth-Century Spain'. *Arizona Journal of Hispanic Cultural Studies* 10 (2006): 151–167.

'*Zarzuela* and the Pastoral'. *Hispanic Issue* 123, no. 8 (2008): 252–273.

Iberni, Luis G., ed. *Ruperto Chapí: Memorias y escritos*. Madrid: Instituto Complutense de Ciencias Musicales, 1995.

Katz, Mark. *Capturing Sound: How Technology Has Changed Music*. Berkeley, CA: University of California Press, 2010.

Kauffman, Deborah. 'Portamento in Romantic Opera'. *Performance Practice Review* 5, no. 2 (1992): 139–158.

Lázaro, Hipólito. *Mi método de canto*. Madrid: Imprenta Agustín Núñez, 1947.

Leech-Wilkinson, Daniel. *The Changing Sound of Music*. London: CHARM, 2009. www.charm.rhul.ac.uk/studies/chapters/.

'Portamento and Musical Meaning'. *Journal of Musicological Research* 25, nos. 3/4 (2006): 233–261.

Maisonneuve, Sophie. 'La Voix de son Maître : Entre corps et technique, l'avènement d'une écoute musicale nouvelle au XXe siècle'. *Communications* 81 (2007): 47–59.

Mejías García, Enrique. 'La correspondencia de los bufos (1871): Ideología de un teatro musical divertido en una España en transformación'. *Revista de Musicología*, 31, no. 1 (2008): 125–149.

'Dinámicas transnacionales en el teatro musical popular: Jacques Offenbach, compositor de zarzuelas (1855–1905)'. PhD thesis, Universidad Complutense de Madrid, 2018.

'Las raíces de la opereta española: Los dos ciegos de Barbieri y Offenbach'. In *La zarzuela y sus caminos: Del siglo XVII a la actualidad*, edited by Tobias Brandenberger and Antje Dreyer, 97–120. Berlin: Lit Verlag, 2016.

Membrez, Nancy J. 'The Teatro Por Horas: History, Dynamics and Comprehensive Bibliography of a Madrid Industry, 1867–1922'. PhD thesis, University of Michigan, 1987.

Molina, Jacinto. *Ataúlfo Argenta: Un año de ausencia*. San Sebastián: Fábrica de Discos Columbia, 1959.

Montero Alonso, José. *Ataúlfo Argenta*. Santander: La Moderna, 1959.

Moral Ruiz, Carmen del. *El género chico: Ocio y teatro en Madrid (1880–1910)*. Madrid: Alianza, 2004.

Morales Villar, María del Coral. 'Los tratados de canto en España durante el siglo XIX: Técnica vocal e interpretación de la música lírica'. PhD thesis, University of Granada, 2008.

Moreda Rodríguez, Eva. 'Amateur Recording on the Phonograph in *fin-de-siècle* Barcelona: Practices, Repertoires and Performers in the Regordosa-Turull Wax Cylinder Collection'. *Journal of the Royal Musical Association* 145, no. 2 (2020): 385–415.

Inventing the Recording: The Phonograph and National Culture in Spain, 1877–1914. New York: Oxford University Press, 2021.

'Reconstructing Zarzuela Performance Practices ca. 1900: Wax Cylinder and Gramophone Disc Recordings of *Gigantes y cabezudos*'. *Journal of Musicology* 37, no. 4 (2020): 459–487.

'Recording *zarzuela grande* in Spain in the Early Days of the Phonograph and Gramophone'. In *Music, Nation and Region in the Iberian Peninsula*, edited by Samuel Llano, Matthew Machin-Autenrieth and Salwa Castelo-Branco, *please add page numbers*. Champaign, IL: University of Illinois Press, 2023.

'Singing and Speaking in Early Twentieth-Century Zarzuela: The Evidence from Early Recordings'. *Journal of Musicological Research* 41, no. 1 (2022): 23–49.

Muñoz, Matilde. *Historia de la zarzuela y el género chico*. Madrid: Tesoro, 1946.

Peña y Goñi, Antonio. *La ópera española y la música dramática en España en el siglo XIX: Apuntes históricos.* Madrid: Instituto Complutense de Ciencias Musicales, 2003 [facsimile of original 1885 edition].

Peres da Costa, Neal. *Off the Record: Performing Practices in Romantic Piano Playing.* New York: Oxford University Press, 2012.

Plack, Rebecca. 'The Substance of Style. How Singing Creates Sound in Lieder Recordings 1902–1939'. PhD thesis, Princeton University, 2008.

Potter, John. 'Beggar at the Door: The Rise and Fall of Portamento in Singing'. *Music and Letters* 87, no. 4 (2006): 523–550.

Potter, Sarah. 'Changing Vocal Style and Technique in Britain during the Long Nineteenth Century'. PhD thesis, University of Leeds, 2014.

Redondo, Marcos. *Un hombre que se va.* Barcelona: Planeta, 1973.

Regidor Arribas, Ramón. *La voz en la zarzuela.* Madrid: Real Musical, 1991.

Rodríguez Arnáez, José Manuel. *Lucrecia Arana: Jarrera castiza – La reina de las tiples del género chico.* Haro: Asociación Cultural Manuel Bartolomé Cossío, 1992.

Salaün, Serge. 'Cuplé y variedades (1890–1915)'. In *La escena española en la encrucijada (1890–1910),* edited by Serge Salaün, Evelyne Ricci and Marie Salgues, 125–151. Madrid: Espiral Hispanoamericana, 2005.

Les espectacles en Espagne. Paris: Presses Sorbonne Nouvelle, 2011.

Sánchez, Víctor. *Tomás Bretón: Un músico de la Restauración.* Madrid: Instituto Complutense de Ciencias Musicales, 2002.

Sorozábal, Pablo. *Mi vida, mi obra.* Madrid: Fundación Banco Exterior, 1986.

Spottswood, Richard. *Ethnic Music on Records: A Discography of Ethnic Recordings Produced in the United States, 1893 to 1942,* vol. 1. Champaign, IL: University of Illinois Press, 1990.

Stanović, Inja and Adam Stanović. 'A Chip Off the Old Block? Introducing the Practice of Historically-Informed Recording'. *Seismograph* (no issue number) (2021), https://seismograf.org/node/19479.

Torres, Elena. 'Zarzuela y musicología: Historia de un debate en permanente revisión'. In *Horizontes de la zarzuela,* edited by Alberto González Lapuente and Alberto Honrado Pinilla, 45–59. Madrid: Fundación Jacinto e Inocencio Guerrero, 2014.

Vendrell, Emili. *El cant (llibre per al cantat i per l'aficionat).* Barcelona: Sucesor de E. Meseguer, 1955.

El mestre Millet i jo: Memòries. Barcelona: Aymà, 1953.

Vendrell Jr, Emili. *El meu pare.* Barcelona: Toray, 1965.

Versteeg, Margot. *De fusiladores y morcilleros: El discurso cómico del género chico (1870–1910).* Amsterdam: Brill, 2010.

Young, Clinton D. *Music Theater and Popular Nationalism in Spain, 1880–1930*. Baton Rouge, LA: Louisiana State University Press, 2016.

'Why Did Spain Fail to Develop Nationalist Opera?' *Bulletin for Spanish and Portuguese Historical Studies* 38, no. 1 (2013): 117–37.

Zurita, Marciano. *Historia del género chico*. Madrid: Prensa Popular, 1920.

Cambridge Elements ⹀

Musical Theatre

William A. Everett
University of Missouri-Kansas City

William A. Everett, PhD is Curators' Distinguished Professor of Musicology at the University of Missouri-Kansas City Conservatory, where he teaches courses ranging from medieval music to contemporary musical theatre. His publications include monographs on operetta composers Sigmund Romberg and Rudolf Friml and a history of the Kansas City Philharmonic Orchestra. He is contributing co-editor of the *Cambridge Companion to the Musical* and the *Palgrave Handbook of Musical Theatre Producers*. Current research topics include race, ethnicity and the musical and London musical theatre during the 1890s.

About the Series

Elements in Musical Theatre focus on either some sort of 'journey' and its resulting dialogue or on theoretical issues. Since many musicals follow a quest model (a character goes in search of something), the idea of a journey aligns closely to a core narrative in musical theatre. Journeys can be, for example, geographic (across bodies of water or land masses), temporal (setting musicals in a different time period than the time of its creation), generic (from one genre to another) or personal (characters in search of some sort of fulfilment). Theoretical issues may include topics relevant to the emerging scholarship on musical theatre from a global perspective and can address social, cultural, analytical and aesthetic perspectives.

Cambridge Elements ≡

Musical Theatre

Printed in the United States
by Baker & Taylor Publisher Services